POET
WARRIOR

POET
WARRIOR

❖

A MEMOIR

❖

JOY HARJO

W. W. NORTON & COMPANY
Independent Publishers Since 1923

For information about permission to reproduce selections from this book,
write to Permissions, W. W. Norton & Company, Inc.,
500 Fifth Avenue, New York, NY 10110

For information about special discounts for bulk purchases, please contact
W. W. Norton Special Sales at specialsales@wwnorton.com or 800-233-4830

Manufacturing by Lake Book
Book design by Beth Steidle
Production manager: Beth Steidle

Library of Congress Cataloging-in-Publication Data
Names: Harjo, Joy, author.
Title: Poet warrior : a memoir / Joy Harjo.
Description: First edition. | New York, N.Y. : W. W. Norton & Company, [2021]
Identifiers: LCCN 2021025215 | ISBN 9780393248524 (hardcover) |
ISBN 9780393248531 (epub)
Subjects: LCSH: Harjo, Joy. | Poets, American—20th century—Biography. |
Poets, American—21st century—Biography. | Indian women authors—
United States—Biography. | LCGFT: Autobiographies. | Autobiographical poetry.
Classification: LCC PS3558.A62423 Z46 2021 | DDC 818/.5403 [B]—dc23
LC record available at https://lccn.loc.gov/2021025215

W. W. Norton & Company, Inc., 500 Fifth Avenue, New York, N.Y. 10110
www.wwnorton.com

W. W. Norton & Company Ltd., 15 Carlisle Street, London W1D 3BS

2 3 4 5 6 7 8 9 0

For the poets, dreamers, visionaries, and risk takers who planted light in the field of darkness so we could rise up

For our children, great-grandchildren, and all those who follow generation by generation in the story of becoming

For the water spider, who, when the earth was covered with water, carried an ember on her back so we could make fire to keep the story going.

For Owen Chopoksa Sapulpa, who walks close to me in the story

Contents

Contents

POET
WARRIOR

To imagine the spirit of poetry is much like imagining the shape and size of the knowing. It is a kind of resurrection light; it is the tall ancestor spirit who has been with me since the beginning, or a bear or a hummingbird. It is a hundred horses running the land in a soft mist, or it is a woman undressing for her beloved in firelight. It is none of these things. It is more than everything.

"You're coming with me, poor thing. You don't know how to listen. You don't know how to speak. You don't know how to sing. I will teach you."

PREPARE

That first earth gift of breathing
Opened your body, these lungs, this heart
Gave birth to the ability to interact
With dreaming
You are a story fed by generations
You carry songs of grief, triumph
Thankfulness and joy
Feel their power as they ascend
Within you
As you walk, run swiftly, even fly
Into infinite possibility

Let go that which burdens you
Let go any acts of unkindness or brutality
From or against you
Let go that which has burdened your family
Your community, your nation
Or disturbed your soul
Let go one breath into another

Pray thankfulness for this Earth we are
For this becoming we are
For this sunlight touching skin we are
For the cooling of the dark we are

Listen now as Earth sheds her skin
Listen as the generations move
One against the other to make power
We are bringing in a new story

We will be accompanied by ancient songs
And will celebrate together

Breathe this new dawn
Assist it as it opens its mouth
To breathe.

＊　＊　＊　＊　＊

You might know me first through a poem, or poetry.
Or you might have heard me speak or sing, or seen my image
    lined up with others who caught attention.
Or I am no one familiar, an anonymous voice through the night
    on the radio, or internet, or in the street calling someone
    home.
Or I'm memory's voice catching your ears when you thought you
    were done with listening.
You might be alone in your room, or in a corner of the house
    where you have made your escape, or in a tree or leaning
    on a rock, and you carry a book, a sketchpad, a pen,
    or a knife—
Or you may have no place at all.
You could be wrapped in rags on the street, detained in a cage at
    a border,
or trapped in other stories of living. Your heart beats out
the human song of survival.
You are looking for words to sustain you, to counter despair.
Come closer so I can feel your breath. You could be my daughter,
    my son. My grandchild or great-grandchild. You might be
    my sister, cousin, uncle, or aunt.

Joy Harjo

In the tradition of the Old Ones, all children are deemed as ours.
We are all related.
Or I am speaking to you in the future, when you are lost in the
    story and
I have crossed the bridge of time into tomorrow.

Part One

❖

ANCESTRAL ROOTS

Girl-Warrior perched on the sky ledge
Overlooking the turquoise, green, and blue garden
Of ocean and earth.
From there she could hear the winds
Lifting from their birthing places
She could hear where sound began.

The winds carried the murmuring of lovers
On Earth to Girl-Warrior's ears—

He was a tall, handsome man whose sensitivity
Was threaded with ancestral love.
He came from tribal leaders who had the humility and heart
To lead through the most difficult striving.
He was water.

She came to his shoulder, her dark auburn hair
Made a halo for her beauty.
She wrote and sang songs that called
What she needed into her hands.
Her heart had room for all growing things,
And she knew her way around a stove.
She was fire.

We want to share all this with a child, they whispered.

The Council dressed Girl-Warrior's spirit for the journey
To enter the story, to make change.
They placed the map in her heart.

You will forget, they told her.
When you ask for our assistance you will find us
In the quiet, in the silent places
Of the earth garden.

Because you are Girl-Warrior you have chosen
A path of many tests. You will learn how to make
Right decisions by making wrong ones.
Those whom you love most will abandon you.
You will find yourself again.

She took a breath, then she was gone.

◆ ◆ ◆ ◆ ◆

I RETURN TO THE STORIES that I was told, the stories that
I can't seem to remember or keep straight to the telling, like the
ones I heard when I used to drive my aunt Lois around the Creek
Nation to visit our relatives—all her age and older, which is the
age I am now. This was when I was in my twenties and thirties,
when she lived in her apartment on West Eighth Street in Okmulgee, before she was disabled with a stroke and taken to a nursing
home to live out the last few years of her life. Every day I miss
her cultural knowledge of our people, her insight and humor. I
miss the historical documents and family artifacts that crowded
her small apartment that told of our family's part in the forced
march from the South to Indian Territory, to what became known
as Oklahoma. These stacks contained written accounts of family stories of bravery and justice, but left out the stories she told
me, of favorite black dogs, horse magic, bending time, how to
avoid the places where known conjurers lived, and of the Spanish

man accompanying the people on the trail, who wore a diamond pin that glittered as he sat tall on his horse. One of her paintings accompanies me through my life since her passing. It is the painting of a Taos man pulling a piece of pottery out of the fire. She used to make many trips to the Southwest and was friends with many of the Pueblo people, including Maria Martinez, the San Ildefonso potter. I am now friends with their grandchildren.

When I was with her, I knew I belonged, and that in this circle of belonging I had a place in the stories. Everyone needs this kind of place, this feeling of kinship; without it we are lost children wandering the earth our whole lives, without a sense of belonging. Even a country can be like a lost child because it may have no roots in the earth on which it has established itself.

I miss being in my aunt's tall physical presence, her graceful and private bearing. Her spiritual presence remains, urging me forward to understanding and love, to knowledge given by her example. She was an artist: a painter, a lover of the arts, of Native arts and cultures. She worked at the Creek Council House and taught art classes in Okmulgee.

Sometimes my aunt was thought of as strange, in the manner that Natives are thought of as strange because they are not effusive in unknown company or have different customs. When I was born, she drove the Okmulgee Beeline to Tulsa to see me, to bring me gifts. My mother puzzled that this aunt of my father's stayed in her car and would not come in. I understand. She was being respectful of my mother. She did not know my mother or of any birth rituals on her side of the family. I am the same way. I will stand apart at the periphery, watching. I might be seen as cold or shy or strange. It has more to do with a kind of sensitivity, honed by experiencing an invading culture and figuring out how best to move to save your life.

Lois Harjo, Artist in Residence, Southern Methodist
University 1935

I am writing in an apartment in downtown Tulsa. I was born
before cell phones and computers, before the proliferation of
devices installed with memory, which prompt the user to forget.
I do not want to forget, though sometimes memory appears to be
an enemy bringing only pain. There are so many memories. One
returned my mother to me. That memory opened up in a dream.
There she was sitting on the roof of a house in red shorts, not

long after she gave birth to me. She was stunning in her youthful health. She was laughing. She was my sun.

I often wish that I had written down everything my aunt and all the elders told me, so I could have their wisdom, their struggles, their hard-won stories right here for referral, to provoke and even cultivate new stories. Growing memories and the ability to access memory is a skill that allows access to eternity. It is within all of us. I do not have the best memory, I often tell the circle of Old Ones when I speak with them—and I do speak with those whom I love who have moved on from this earthly realm, especially when writing poetry or any kind of story or music. They remind me, here's your opportunity to practice memory. I am not the best listener or speaker, I tell them. Take your opportunity with grace, they tell me. You are here to learn, learn how to listen, how to walk into each challenging story without fear, fearless.

I have asked my aunt, uncles, cousins, and others, all those with whom I sat, listened, and shared throughout this life, to be with me as I write. It is a very different world within which you make stories, share, and participate, they tell me.

"Too many words," I heard one sixth great-grandfather remark.

"What is it with you and all these English words?"

These times were predicted, a time in which the birds would be confused about which direction to fly to migrate, a time in which the sun would darken with pollution, a time in which there would be confusion and famine. In these kinds of times, we are in great danger of forgetting our original teachings, the nature of the kind of world we share and what it requires of us. In this world of forgetfulness, they told me, you will forget how to nourish the connection between humans, plants, animals, and the elements, a connection needed to make food for your mind, heart, body, and spirit. You were born of a generation that promised to help remember. Each generation makes a person. You came in together to make change.

They tell me that if I had come into their houses with pen and paper or recorder, sat on their porches or at the table drinking iced tea, writing instead of listening, I would have made myself a stranger, separating myself from the story. Too many with pens poised over paper wrote down laws that robbed millions of acres of our lands, that stole children, homes, and legacies. That part of our history is still going on, they said, and now, like then, they use our tribal members and relatives for their work to divide the people and steal. They will not be satisfied until everything is gone. Native peoples will be here when they are done, and when the earth and waters are renewed.

Life never goes in a straight line in our Native communities. Time moves slower. Someone might ask us to sit down and eat, or another cousin could go in the back room to get the medicine we need, their gnarled brown hands carefully folding the top of the paper bag with the roots that have Creek names and songs. Or someone might tell a memory that would bring everyone together in tears and laughter, or the memory of someone passed would rise up in that song.

They all agreed that we are being brought to a place where we will once again remember how to speak with animals, plants, and life forms. We will once again know our humble place as two-legged humans. Humans are not the only ones with a spirit, they reminded. Nor are we more important than everyone else.

And besides, they laughed, if you had written everything down, you wouldn't have been able to read your handwriting any-way. We sure can't read anything you write longhand.

Joy Harjo

We always laugh, even about the worst. That's when we laugh hardest.

And, they added, we were telling these stories for each other, not to be put in a book. However, times have changed. We resisted change because so much has been needlessly destroyed. We are fiercely protective of those teachings that were given to us. However, we must adapt.

◆　◆　◆　◆　◆

The Old Ones opened the ears of Girl-Warrior
Tempering the frequency before she left
On her mission.
We are sending you, they said,
To learn how to listen.
There is good in this world.
There is evil.
There is no story without one and the other.
You will be gravity.
You will be feather.
Send each story to the heart,
Each word before you act or speak.

◆　◆　◆　◆　◆

WHEN MY AUNT LOIS AND I used to visit our cousin George Coser Sr., my favorite stories were often about our great-grandfather Monahwee, one of the beloved leaders of our people, a man who with his warriors stood up against Andrew Jackson and the U.S. government against the illegal move from our homelands. The story did not end in triumph. The bodies of our warriors, women, and children littered the grassy curves of Horseshoe Bend of the Tallapoosa River. Monahwee's first wife and children were killed there along with hundreds of others, by Jackson, his troops and allies. We did not have the numbers, guns, or laws to stand up to the immigrants who believed that everything of the earth was given to them because they were God's chosen people.

Some of the survivors went south with Seminole and Miccosukee. Others, like Monahwee, went west with their families, crossed the Mississippi to Indian Territory to where they were promised peace. A few stayed because their loyalties shifted. Half did not make it. They were killed by sickness, the leaving, the heartbreak.

I've read personal historical accounts that assert that Monahwee never made it to Indian Territory, that he died in Alabama or somewhere unknown on the trail. The emigration records tell a different story. We have the map of his journey on the Trail of Tears to Indian Territory. He and his family traveled with the Fish Pond Mekko and his family from Talladega, Alabama. The emigration agent wrote of his frustration when his charges wouldn't keep to a schedule. They were somewhere along the Arkansas River camped outside Memphis. As the agent urged departure, Monahwee refused to leave because he was having one of his legendary parties. His parties often went on for days.

Before removal, our people were walking the tightrope of history. Immigrants were flooding illegally into our homelands, staking claims to our lands and houses even as we occupied them. Tecumseh had come down to the South and met with our warriors. The Red Stick warriors aligned with Tecumseh in an attempt to hold on to home and culture, to make a stand for what rightfully belonged in our care. There was much negotiating going on over every kind of human transaction. The community needed some relief.

Joy Harjo

Monahwee decided to have a celebration for his warriors in his camp, when one afternoon an Indian agent from Washington, D.C., arrived on horseback on official business. He was sweaty in his wool uniform as he walked up to Monahwee's home. Monahwee told his warriors that he would be right back, as he pulled a light deerskin wrap over his shoulder. He excused himself from the party to speak with the officer. I can hear some of the warriors singing drinking songs. I hear laughter and can smell the sputter of meat cooking over a fire. Monahwee was very polite with the government official, telling him, in the official manner of English that he had learned from government officials, that he was conducting business with his warriors and to please come back in four days. At that moment some of the warriors could be heard whooping, making *yahke* cries, probably louder than usual, specifically for the agent's ears. The agent protested, as he had ridden for more than a few days to get there, and he had other business in the area. Monahwee called a younger warrior to take care of the agent's horse, directed the agent to the cooking house, then turned back to join his party of warriors.

I consider that a healing story. It heals the stereotype of Natives greeting visitors with the word "how" and woodenly shaking hands as if they were mascots, primitives without manners and not human beings.

❖   ❖   ❖   ❖   ❖

I KNOW WHERE MONAHWEE IS buried. My cousin "Porky," or John Scott, showed me one afternoon as we drove around Creek country, visiting the places of the stories that were passed to us to remember. We drove past Hanna toward Eufaula to find the place. There is a small Creek family cemetery back in those roads. There most graves are covered with traditional spirit houses. In the back, in a flat area, is where Monahwee is buried. There is no tombstone or spirit house. Seven cedar trees surround his humble gravesite.

◆ ◆ ◆ ◆ ◆

MY COUSIN DONA JO HARJO-WEBB grew up in Okemah and was a champion barrel-racer. We became close in her later years. She fled Oklahoma for California and that's where I found her, not far from Chico in Live Oak. She and my father were close cousins. They were both marked by a similar restlessness and independence, something I inherited. She and I picked up where they had left off. At night in her little house with a black walnut tree in the back we sipped wine while her pet pigeon, Pidge, hopped back and forth in his cage on one leg. We could talk about anything. We shared the same deep voice, which was the same voice of the aunt we loved most, our aunt Lois. She was always included in our conversations, always referenced. We shared the same love of horses and animals. Dona Jo told me that she used to wake up from dreaming crying out the name "Monahwee, Monahwee." I had to tell her who he was, of his horsemanship, and we wondered at her waking up with his name crying out from her sleep. We discussed how history lives within us, even if we don't know it. How even something like daring is passed forward because it needs a place to live.

A family is essentially a field of stories, each intricately connected. Death does not sever the connection; rather, the story expands as it continues unwinding inter-dimensionally. Monahwee was with us as we spoke because speaking woke up the memory. He was with us in dreaming even though he had passed as an old man in Indian Territory. I am here speaking with you now, even as you are there. I am here even as I might be in the hereafter years later from you being here, now, in this word field. When we look at the sky, we are seeing the future because it is so far away, though scientists would argue you cannot see the future because it is not happening yet. They affirm that we are seeing the past when we observe the occupants of the night sky. According to the Old Ones, it is all occurring now. Time is a weave, like a DNA spiral moving within, through us, and around us. It is always changing.

Dona Jo's father was gone before I was born. He was the brother of my grandmother Naomi and aunt Lois. For some reason Uncle Joe likes to be around me and continues to check in. Everyone with sight sees him with me. I see how I must invoke curiosity in these relatives. They are watching to see how I will fulfill their promises, their dreams.

Dona Jo had one daughter, Tiffany. Never was anyone so unsuited for such a name that invokes diamonds, lamps, and sparkling fine things. Tiffany was big-shouldered and butch. She was in her forties when she went to prison for driving a getaway car for a small-time robbery. Drugs must have been involved, as she would die not long after she got out of prison, the second time for violating parole, from an infected needle wound in her thigh from shooting up.

When Tiffany was in prison we wrote back and forth. She wrote that she was tired of carrying the burden of her past. I had materials sent to her to write her story, as a method of getting at the pain that was haunting her. I would be a witness, I told her. Write without censoring. If there were any stories that she didn't want me to read, to write it anyway and staple the pages together.

I would not read them. This was about bringing everything to the surface so it could be let go and have no more power over her.

From prison, my cousin sent me packets of pages and pages of stories. Many of the stories occurred in the first fourteen years of her life when she was a child in Okemah. There was page after page of handwritten emotional prose detailing sexual abuse and other violence as she grew older, documenting a lost trail through failed relationships. It was quite a catalog of abuse and addictive behavior.

We are all here to serve each other. At some point we have to understand that we do not need to carry a story that is unbearable. We can observe the story, which is mental; feel the story, which is physical; let the story go, which is emotional; then forgive the story, which is spiritual, after which we use the materials of it to build a house of knowledge.

Tiffany and her mother Dona Jo passed from this life within a month of each other. I was flying back and forth from Albuquerque to check on Dona Jo, who was becoming more and more incapacitated. She had diabetes and it was becoming harder for her to walk because of her weight. She began to rely on a wheelchair, then was in and out of the hospital while Tiffany was in and out of prison.

Something strange happened during that time. I had rented a car in Sacramento to drive north to Marysville to see Dona Jo in the hospital. It was dusk as I drove the two-lane through almond orchards and the tall and fragrant eucalyptus trees. Dona had worked the last years of her life on the line in the factories, sorting nuts from these orchards. Suddenly a white owl swooped down, nearly touching the windshield of my car. I knew this was no accidental occurrence.

Birds are messengers. The owl gives very distinct messages,

often about transformations in our lives. They do not necessarily mean death. They represent spiritual power. Power can be dangerous. Power can give or take life.

Then, a week later after the incident with the owl, I was being driven in a car in Montana to a performance in a Native community. It was the first dark just after dusk. A white owl came down and swooped across the windshield, this time, on the passenger side, where I was sitting.

I sat up and made note. I did not know exactly what it meant, and it is not always meant for us to know. The wing resonance drew a feeling in the wind. I felt the approach of death.

Then, there was another owl.

Within a month, Tiffany died suddenly of her infection. Dona Jo passed in the hospital as everyone in the country celebrated a false story of settlers and Natives having dinner together, when in reality Native heads were on pikes surrounding the settler community who were feasting on what they had been taught to plant by the Native people. Though at that moment I was far away in New Mexico, I felt my cousin's soul lift from her body as she was taken home.

Shortly after these burials, putting-away ceremonies and grieving, I was home, driving east on the interstate. Without the warning, planted by the third owl, I would not have thought to look in the rearview mirror in enough time to get out of the way of a drugged-out driver who was speeding directly toward the back of my vehicle. I could have been killed without the prescient message.

The owls don't always appear just to warn. I saw a white owl at the side of the road once while driving to Isleta. It was hunting. It wasn't my messenger. They are not always on duty.

And now usually when they appear to me, to warn, they do so

in dreams. Once I saw an owl far off on the female, or left, side. I tried not to see it. It was telling me that a female who was not closely related to me would be passing. I pretended not to see the owl, to ward it off. In response it came over and stood directly in front of me. I had to laugh, to dream laugh.

◆　◆　◆　◆　◆

Girl-Warrior began to notice
She was different.
When asked a question, even a simple question
Maybe, about a pine tree in memory,
She could not respond in a straight line.
She might see a pine tree. Then a row of pine trees.
Then the history of pine trees,
Or from the point of view of a pine tree,
or the dream of a pine tree far from the earth and the sky
all upon being asked the question.

By then, she did not know how to respond.
She was lost in an eternity of pine trees.
Her instinct was to build in circles
When asked a question.
She might lose the beginning
And then the ending.
She might have the start of a painting
Or a poem
But no easy yes or no response.

◆　◆　◆　◆　◆

Joy Harjo

ONE AFTERNOON IN WEST HOLLYWOOD I decided to follow a thought made of words. I had just finished a spin biking class and was toweling off when I thought: "I want a doughnut." I imagined it glistening with sugar glaze. Its appearance in my mind did not quite fit. I had not eaten doughnuts for years. I followed the thought to the biker next to me. It was not my thought; it was the biker's thought. I began to follow all of my thoughts and was surprised how many didn't belong to me. And how many had threads to ancestors, relatives, strangers, even plants, elements, and animals.

❖　❖　❖　❖　❖

MY MOTHER WAS A TALKER. Everyone knew my mother. She was friendly and moved about the earth collecting stories with a natural curiosity. She loved words, especially the way they could move with music. My mother had an eighth-grade education, which gave her a great insecurity about words. Yet in her songwriting, as in the poetry she loved, words could grow wings. They could fly.

My mother made friends wherever she went in the neighborhood: the market, the local bar where she was the shuffleboard queen, or the beauty shop. She was a good-looking woman and men at every age were attracted. Women were her best friends. My mother was the one who kept a party going, and she was one of the best bakers, so these gatherings usually happened in our kitchen. She kept the kitchen spotless. Everything shined. Even the sunlight preferred my mother's kitchen over all the others in the kingdom of kitchens. The sun entered happily through the windows cleaned with vinegar, framed by large, green-leafed plants.

When my mother and her girlfriends started getting serious with their talk and I was shooed out of the kitchen, I hid. I perfected the art of disappearance. I'd appear to leave, then slide quietly beneath the kitchen table. I can still feel the curve of the table legs, how they met in the middle and branched out, made a circle into which I fit perfectly, beneath the ebb and flow of women-talk. My ears were bent for stories, for the forbidden, the mystery pieces. It was there I heard who was pregnant, found out the neighbor was a bootlegger, and knew my best friend was moving even before she did. A story could destroy someone's life or make someone else a hero. This story circle was a powerful place.

My mother would share, of course, but never for pity. She was positive and never complained, no matter how difficult her struggle. My father had hit on most of these women but if any of them had succumbed they were not in the circle. My mother could smell them out. Her sense of knowing was honed to a blade of difficult truth. Because of that, of course, she knew I was under the table. She understood it, as she too was the consummate story gatherer. And I was, after all, my mother's daughter.

◆　◆　◆　◆　◆

PERHAPS THE WORLD ENDS HERE

The world begins at a kitchen table. No matter what, we must eat to live.

The gifts of earth are brought and prepared, set on the table.
So it has been since creation, and it will go on.

　　　　　　　　　　　　　　　　　Joy Harjo

We chase chickens or dogs away from it. Babies teethe at the
    corners.
They scrape their knees under it.

It is here that children are given instructions on what it means to be
human. We make men at it, we make women.

At this table we gossip, recall enemies and the ghosts of lovers.

Our dreams drink coffee with us as they put their arms around our
children. They laugh with us at our poor falling-down selves and as
we put ourselves back together once again at the table.

This table has been a house in the rain, an umbrella in the sun.

Wars have begun and ended at this table. It is a place to hide in the
shadow of terror. A place to celebrate the terrible victory.

We have given birth on this table, and have prepared our
parents for burial here.

At this table we sing with joy, with sorrow. We pray of suffering
and remorse. We give thanks.

Perhaps the world will end at the kitchen table, while we are
    laughing
and crying, eating of the last sweet bite.

❖   ❖   ❖   ❖   ❖

MY MOTHER WAS MY FIRST teacher.

I can hear my mother reciting from William Blake, when I am not much more than knee-length:

"Little lamb who made thee / Dost though know who made thee / Gave thee life and bid thee feed / By the stream and o'er the mead . . ."

This was the first poem I learned. It was more than the words. It was how the words locked into a pleasing rhythm and we would move to them, and how like a lamb frolicking in spring, the words danced across the tongue. I didn't know what the words "frolicking" or "mead" meant, but it didn't matter as the sound and rhythm made something new that I wanted to engage in. It was about my mother speaking in a manner that was beyond ordinary. It was about my mother passing love to me as she spoke music into my ears.

In the late seventies, I was invited to Amsterdam in the Netherlands for a world poetry festival. It was my first journey out of the country. I performed with many others at the festival, poets from all over the world. I sat in a packed auditorium and heard the dub poet Linton Kwesi Johnson read his poetry solo, without his band. As we swayed together at the patois phrasing of his recitation, I remembered my mother, William Blake, and me.

❖　❖　❖　❖　❖

MY MOTHER AND HER MOTHER did not get along. My mother was her father's favorite, the only girl of six brothers, and could get almost anything by her father, in defiance of her mother. She

　　　　　　　　　　　　　　　　　　　Joy Harjo

was his flower, a rose, like the roses she planted all around the yard of her last home before her passing. After she was gone that October, all her roses bloomed through winter and kept blooming into the fall of the next year. That was our mother.

◆ ◆ ◆ ◆ ◆

I HAVE TOLD SOME OF these stories many times, and you may have heard some or most of them already. Memory can compress and expand. Arms and legs can stick out. Some stories are demanding. They will find no rest until they are told once more, like a child wanting to hear the same story over and over again, even though they know how it's going to end. The stories tap you on the shoulder, pull at your shirt, begging for attention again. The more years you gather, the more stories you have that want to be retold. But it's the same ones that often haunt you. It's why we return to our childhood home over and over again in memory, to the same rooms, the same lands, the same songs on the radio.

When I was a child, I liked hearing how my mother worked the picking fields, how she could pick green beans or strawberries quicker than almost anyone, and how she saved enough money to run away from home, against her father's will, with her friend Elvira Guerra. She met my father and that was it. He blazed with charisma and sensuality. He courted her on the famous dance floors of Tulsa, and they married. There I was exactly nine months later. My brother followed eighteen months after, and then the other two children, one after another. My parents' origin story was the torch that kept her going through the downfall from the impossible dream of eternal, sugar-coated romance sold to teen-agers, to women everywhere.

My mother carried a great pride. There was much she would not speak or reveal to anyone. She had come a long way from her beginnings of dire poverty and did not want shame to determine her value. She had accomplished what she set out to do: she had a home of her own, she had a good-looking husband with a steady job, and she had the four children she had dreamed of to seal her happiness.

◆ ◆ ◆ ◆ ◆

IT WAS SUMMER. I NOTED that my father appeared freer in the warmer months. He wore short sleeves. I liked his deeper brown skin. My father did not feel compelled to speak much at all until he was in the company of his friends or drinking. Usually, these occasions occurred at the same time. He was not a man of words, though he was an educated Muscogee Creek man who grew up in a twenty-one-room house, a house bought by oil money, and his mother came from a line of respected warriors, and speakers who served the tribal nation in the House of Warriors.

I began to pay close attention to what he said as he walked about the house and out to the garage where he worked on his cars, his pickup. I often followed him around because I loved assisting him with tools, though he could be impatient with me, even abrupt. The intriguing word that summer was "bullshit." He used that word often when he worked and when he kicked back with his friends. I didn't know the meaning of this word so curious to my ears. I liked the punch of it. I decided to try the word out when my father was gathered with his friends around the coffee table in the living room. I toddled in. I was that young. And in imitation of my father, I exclaimed, "Bullshit!" I expected him to be proud of me for repeating this word.

His friends thought it was funny until he threw me against the wall.

When I stood up after being thrown, I felt ashamed. Shame originates in the knot of your sacral root and climbs up the rest of your body, like a hate-smelling smoke. I discovered it can linger for years. Even generations.

I did not stop my word finding. I just did it alone under the table or in the closet in the small bedroom that housed us four children. That closet was my refuge. I decorated it with drawings and words in crayon and chalk.

I loved words. How they felt in my mouth. I would taste them. Sing them. I would experiment saying them over and over, frontward and backward, for the way sound felt in my mouth and ears, and for the rhythms as they moved through my body. This was a quiet ritual, when I was alone.

"Aggravate," "tomato," "bastard," "robin" were some of the words I would repeat over and over to myself.

I was learning that speaking was fraught with consequences. And fear was planted in me before I could speak, from my father's violence.

I learned from my mother that this silencing started long before the word "bullshit." She told me of how when I was an infant, she was up in the night trying to get me to sleep. I cried and cried because I had colic. I was being bottle-fed cow's milk and was lactose intolerant, but no one knew about that in those times. One night during a crying bout, my father approached us and bent close. Someone watching might think he came to cradle both of us in his arms in a gesture of tenderness. Then he told my mother, in that intimate circle, to shut that baby up or he would kill me.

◆ ◆ ◆ ◆ ◆

HERE IS A LULLABY FOR that baby who was my father, whose mother died when he was still nursing, when he was left bereft and cried and cried, until his father shut him up.

Beautiful baby, beautiful child
Hokosucē herosē. Estuce herosē.
Beautiful baby, beautiful child.
Hokosucē herosē, Estuce herosē.
The sky is your blanket; the earth is your cradle.
Sutvt vccetv cēnakēt os. Ekvnv cen topv hakes.
Your mother rocks you close to her heart.
Ceckē ēfekkē temposen ce haneces.

My father, Allen W. Foster, Jr., as a boy

Joy Harjo

Your father holds up the sky.
Cerkē sutv hvlwen kvwapes.
Beautiful baby, beautiful child.
Hokosucē herosē, Estuce herosē.

◆　◆　◆　◆　◆

In those earliest years Girl-Warrior
Spoke freely with the earth
And the plants, the animals
That roamed in the yard of the small house
Where her family lived.
She was most herself when she was alone
And could hear the thrumming curiosity
Of the Creator who was pleased
With creation

Baby brown-skinned girl
Patted out mud circles
And fed them to her friends
The frogs, the horny toads,
The roly-poly bugs
Even the bees who would alight
Before they flew off to find sweetness
To make more sweetness.

Far away, inside the house,
Girl-Warrior's parents partied
With their friends,
They had fun.
Then they fought.

Then her father left.
Then he came back.
Then he caught her mother in his grip.
When he drank,
His words sparked and shined.
Only then, could he speak.

✦ ✦ ✦ ✦ ✦

I TRIED TO TELL MY mother about what happened many nights, after everyone had gone to sleep. How I could lift up from my sleeping body, would see it wrapped in its blanket, still on the army cot. How I could then walk through walls, and go see her and my father sleeping in their room beneath the chenille bedspread, and then walk the neighborhood, visiting the various dog friends I had made. How I could then fly into places all over and visit people from long ago. I tried to explain to her, but I would get frustrated at not having the right words to tell what I had seen and experienced.

I flew to lands far away, and ancient times in those lands. We did not have books in our house with those kinds of images. I traveled to underwater worlds, to many places. Some were made of colorful, geometric shapes and there were no words.

I found refuge with the Old Ones of our people. I didn't always return with their words, stories, or images in conscious memory, but they were stored deep within. The meanings emerged at different ages, exactly when I needed them.

In the mornings as I ate my cereal, eggs, or pancakes I'd tell my mother my stories.

"You have quite the imagination, baby," she might say.

"It really happened; it was not just a dream," I would respond to my mother, knowing that neither she nor anyone else would

My brother, Allen, my mother, and me

believe me. I learned not to say anything of what I was dreaming or seeing. I felt a frustrating gap between the earthly childmind and the mind not bound by time or space.

As a child, I drew and drew some of these images. And when grown, I would come to find expression of what was unspeakable in the arts, in music and in poetry.

◆　◆　◆　◆　◆

Girl-Warrior followed blue
To comprehend what it meant exactly—
There was black night blue that you had to hold to the light
The meaning mystery, or bruised—
Or her mother crying while she mopped the kitchen floor
Digging into the corners on her hands and knees.
Or was it her father coming home at dawn when the sky
Was turning from black to sun-in-the-sky blue?
He'd come for her and she wouldn't know whether to run
To his arms or hide—he'd throw her to the sky blue
When he was happy or if he was blue, he'd be mean.
Elvis Presley sang "Don't Be Cruel" for her father
All the way to the edge of eternity blue
To where blue is not possible except in a song with a few guitars
And a drummer.
"I give myself to blue winds"
Sang the bird with blue in its mouth—
The one Girl-Warrior was drawing
To give her mother, who wouldn't believe her story of blue
Because she had no place, no time for such a foolish
Daughter, always making things up.
Girl-Warrior stood to wash dishes on a chair
Singing blue along with the singers who were tiny
And lived in the radio
Perched on the shelf above the sink.

When she sang with them everywhere it was blue.

* * * * *

Joy Harjo

DURING SECOND GRADE MY MOTHER was out of the house waitressing at a truck stop over on Admiral Street, and our household was growing more and more chaotic with my father and his drinking and women. We had a string of babysitters. One of my favorite babysitters had a long coat I liked to wear. It was a soft, light wool. Even at that age I could tell that it was made well, not from the places we bought our school clothes. We also got many of our clothes from boxes of outgrown items that were passed around among my mother and her friends.

As I speak, I can almost see the tag at the neck, the stitched edging in gold thread of the babysitter's coat. I pulled the coat on. Though the sleeves extended a distance from my hands, and the coat hem dragged behind me, I felt elegant. My brother saw my self-satisfaction and pushed me. I chased him. We began roughhousing and I took off again and ran around the room. He stepped on the hem of the coat and I went flying. I chipped a front permanent tooth.

A few weeks later as I sat reading silently in class the nerve in the tooth began throbbing. I would not speak in school or otherwise put myself forward. If I told the teacher my tooth hurt, then they would call my mother where she was working. I knew how much everything cost and knew that if I took her out of work there would be less, minus the time it would take to pick me up. My mother would never chide me for it, she was not that way. But I would know. I was her confidante. I knew things that a child should never know or worry about, like the names of the women my father was seeing, what they were doing and where, and how difficult it was to keep the household going. On the other hand, I was often the first one to hear the drafts of the songs she was writing. I was her favorite dance partner, and we would jitterbug wildly around the kitchen during breaks in her cooking, sewing, and writing.

The teacher saw my silent tears and called my mother anyway.

My mother took me to a dental office in a nearby shopping center. I felt bad that it was going to cost her money. I had never been to a dentist until then. In a conference with the dentist, we learned that to pull the tooth was much more cost effective. We did not have the funds for replacing the tooth with a bridge. That afternoon I was put under with gas and my tooth was pulled. I grew into womanhood with a front tooth missing. You have no authority to speak with a tooth-length gap in the front of your mouth. You no longer have value. Any words are ruined before they reach air.

◆ ◆ ◆ ◆ ◆

One night when Girl-Warrior was out traveling
In dreaming time, she went looking for the fire.
That's where the Old Ones sat and watched
And looked after those who were left behind
In the Earth story.
She stood at the edge and waited respectfully
To be called over.
Fire was friendly and within it many colors
That cannot be found on Earth.
Fire was singing as it rose up
To give back the wisdom of its flames.
Girl-Warrior was motioned in;
She sat down next to her kin.
She listened.
It was the fire that kept her ear turned

Joy Harjo

Toward story.
There was a girl, fire sang
Who left us for Earth,
During star rise.
In her pack she was given poetry.
Every gift has tests
Before they can be opened
To be shared.

◆　◆　◆　◆　◆

IT WAS THAT SAME YEAR I asked for books of poetry for my birthday. I was given Louis Untermeyer's *Golden Treasury of Poetry*. It was there I first found the poet Emily Dickinson. As I perched that large book between my skinned knees, alone in my need to be alone, her voice reached out from the pages and made friends with me. I could hear her, though we were years, miles, landscapes, and cultures away from each other. I liked to read aloud to myself:

I'm Nobody! Who are you?
Are you—Nobody—Too?
Then there's a pair of us!

I was a nobody, hearing the voice of another nobody, both of us peering at each other from behind our knees. We bonded over our hiding places. Two nobodies equal one somebody. Emily's poems told me she too found herself with words. Poetry was a refuge from the instability and barrage of human disappointment. When I read and listened to poetry, I was out of the crossfire of my parents. I never knew when my father would come home, and if he did, what condition he would be in. My mother was in fury or tears as she left for work, sometimes two jobs, and then returned home to cook, clean, and care for her four children. Everything was coming apart and I didn't know what was going to happen to us. There was talk of adopting us children out. There were too many of us, said my father. My mother would not let us go.

I retreated to poetry. I disappeared into the music. Poetry lingered there with me. And when there was music and poetry, dance was not far behind. The dreaming realm worlds were growing dimmer and dimmer as there was no place for them in a world of schoolbooks, classes, and scientific knowledge. But with poetry, doors would open inside even as I heard them slamming, outside.

I was the highwayman in Alfred Noyes's "The Highwayman" galloping through the darkness, with its rhythm and onomatopoeic precision through the looming tragedy of household drama.

The wind was a torrent of darkness among the gusty trees.
The moon was a ghostly galleon tossed upon cloudy seas.
The road was a ribbon of moonlight over the purple moor,
And the highwayman came riding—
    Riding—riding—
The highwayman came riding, up to the old inn-door.

I made myself small or invisible during the outbursts, which were most often late at night, after they'd been to a party and he'd drunk too much and had brazenly put the moves on other women in front of my beautiful mother. One of his conquests he brought into the children's bedroom when we were supposed to be sleeping. I remember their lit cigarettes circling in the dark.

"ribbon of moonlight over the purple moor . . ."

Joy Harjo

We had no purple moors in Oklahoma. I kept a dictionary close to look up words. One summer, I spent learning words in the dictionary and practicing them. I started with the letter "a" and went from there. There were so many "a's," I didn't make it past them.

The built-up simmer of anger would spill over to the morning and sometimes the party would start all over early in the afternoon. I would disappear under the covers or flee into my hiding place in the closet or under the table. The rhythms of poetry brought me into a circle, like the rhythms of the elders talking and telling stories that always brought me back to the fire that warmed my soul.

◆　◆　◆　◆　◆

"YOU ARE A LATE BLOOMER," my mother always reminded me. I was born two months premature. "It takes early born children longer to catch up," she would say. "You were on a ventilator."

"What's a ventilator?" I'd ask, even though I knew the answer. I loved the sound of the word, which sounded like itself, the in and out of breath being forced in and out of my lungs to keep me living.

"When the doctor took you off the ventilator you were given minutes to learn how to breathe on your own."

I was a late breather. I decided to stay.

I didn't begin to walk until I was thirteen months. I began speaking long past the time children normally begin speaking.

Now that I am much older, I wonder if I am still dragging just a little behind others of my age.

I have a tendency to hold back, to watch, to wait until I have clarity, a sure path.

✦ ✦ ✦ ✦ ✦

AS MUCH AS I LOVED poetry, I often felt alone in my love. Being a poet was nothing anyone could aspire to be. There were no poets in our neighborhood, a community that included many Creek, Cherokee, Osage, and Seminole citizens. That didn't mean that there weren't poets in our communities or that we didn't have poets in our tribal histories. One of the most nationally well-known and well-published poets from Oklahoma from the borderlands of the late nineteenth and early twentieth century was Alexander Posey. Posey was from Eufaula, where many of my relatives lived. My aunt Lois said we were related. I believe I remember her saying it was through her grandmother Miley (Millie) Carr, who married David Monahwee. It was her family.

Posey lived during a time of great change as the Muscogee Creek people transitioned through many shifts of fortune—the worst probably being the passing of the Dawes Act, or Allotment Act, a U.S. government act that instituted one of the largest land thefts by parceling tribal land for private ownership, then giving away a vast majority of it to non-Native people. Posey was directly involved, as an agent. He founded the first daily tribal newspaper in the nation, the *Eufaula Indian Journal*. He wrote about the dissolution of tribal governments and the dismantling of tribal lands. His *Fus Fixico Letters* were written from a fictional voice of local wit, wisdom, and dialect of a tribal citizen of our Creek Nation. Posey's poetry was more personal in voice, in subject, even as he grappled with the same issues he confronted in his journalism. He died at age thirty-four by drowning, which he foretold in this poem.

MY FANCY

Why do trees along the river
  Lean so far out o'er the tide?
Very wise men tell me why, but
  I am never satisfied;
And so I keep my fancy still,
  That trees lean out to save
The drowning from the clutches of
  The cold, remorseless wave.

When I re-read Posey's poem "Assured," I imagine it is spirit food for young poets and artists trying to figure out the path of becoming a poet when there appears to be none. I imagine myself the ages of my grandchildren, taking this poem to heart when the future doesn't feel so assured. In the poem, we all stand up in the flickering of life that can only happen with dark and bright, pain and rest, wrong and right, and the worst and the best.

ASSURED

Be it dark; be it bright;
  Be it pain; be it rest;
Be it wrong; be it right—
  It must be for the best.
Some good must somewhere wait,
  And sometime joy and pain
Must cease to alternate,
  Or else we live in vain.

In the public schools I attended, we did not find any of Alexander Posey's poetry in our books. We were taught poetry in our elementary and junior high school classes once a year during the dreaded poetry unit. We would be asked by teachers, who were often lost when it came to poetry, questions like:

"What did this poet from England a century ago mean when they said . . . ?"

Yes, what did it mean?, we'd wonder in confused silence.

Or we would be asked to scan the meter when we were unsure of accents in the stylized language of a century or two ago.

Poetry, when taught this way, was an irrelevant stranger to our ears, when we naturally made poetry on the playground, jumped rope to it.

We were not taught how this poetry could bring rain, turn the heart of a lover, speak truth in a dying country, undo the rein of a dictator. Or what in the poem gave it that kind of power. We did not know how poetry lived in our tribal communities, often sung or in the language of speeches and speaking, doing the hard work of ritual.

We could have been taught to listen.

I imagine being in an elementary or middle school classroom and hearing the teacher urging us to:

Listen with your ears, your eyes, your throat, your abdomen, your toes . . .

I am right there. We can listen with everything. Imagine listening with your belly to the cricket on the stairs, the raven at the door.

Then, let's discuss the historic period of the poem, the kind of language and how it evolved and why, and what was going on culturally. We will view images of the land and plants, then we will go back and listen again.

We can listen the way we would listen to a song, for ear pleasure. The gates of poetry would open wide, and we'd have something we absolutely needed for our pre-adolescent lives in which we'd see a president shot live on television, watch bloody skirmishes in Vietnam, the protests for racial justice, or the emergence of so-called "free love." And never did we see indigenous people, in any kind of written or media story. We only appeared in the story field as hunted by the U.S. Cavalry, romanticized as speakers of short syllabic words of simple truths, or inspirers of fashion in the beads and bandanas of hippies. We were not poets.

Instead, in those years back then, we'd labor through poetry, when poetry had many gifts to share, and then to the next unit of study, even worse, to sentence diagramming.

◆　◆　◆　◆　◆

Girl-Warrior was lonely
For the poetry-talk of the Old Ones.
They spoke in metaphor,
A way of language that alerted her imagination
To the presence of mystery
Where there was always a light on in the mica windows
Of her soul's house
Where knowledge did not depend on words
Of faulty human languages.

In one of time's rooms, a place she liked to visit
She played, as all babies do, with sunlight on her fingers.

She was a tiny weaver, a dreamer.
The Old Ones always gather around the baskets
Holding the little ones,
Admiring them, reminding them
Of their legacy of honor and beauty
Each one of them, all colors, all sizes,
All cultural expressions, all creations
Worthy of love.

◆ ◆ ◆ ◆ ◆

AS I NEAR THE LAST doorway of my present life, I am trying to understand the restless path on which I have traveled. My failures have been my most exacting teachers. They are all linked by one central characteristic, and that is the failure to properly regard the voice of inner truth. That voice speaks softly. It is not judgmental, full of pride, or otherwise loud. It does not deride, shame, or otherwise attempt to derail you. When I fail to trust what my deepest knowing tells me, then I suffer. The voice of inner truth, or the knowing, has access to the wisdom of eternal knowledge. The perspective of that voice is timeless.

I would never have become a poet if I hadn't listened to that small, inner voice that told me that poetry was the path, even when I had different plans. All of the other voices of educators and friends, voices of love and concern told me that poetry was an impossible vocation. They reminded me I had two small children to raise alone, that I should change my major to education, then I could teach poetry if I wanted to be invested in poetry. Instead, I listened to that humble voice that did not need to puff itself up or have approval to be chosen.

I have made choices that made no sense to anyone else, but

they were the right choices for me. I didn't always understand them either; even the choice to be a poet is still often a mystery, just as is the need to create and make music. When I listen, I am always led in the right direction. That doesn't mean the resultant path is easy. It might be the more difficult path. You may have to clear boulders, walk through fire after fire, or try to find footing in precarious flooding. You will play the wrong notes and write words that mean nothing to anyone else but you. And you may appear to have followed the wrong path even though it was the right path, as you fail over and over again.

I remain very aware of my failures and often run them obsessively through my mind, which is a failure in and of itself. If I let them go, they can run on their own track until they wear themselves out to nothing. It's better to tend to cultivating knowledge, to learn from all of the many teachers who are part of the catalog of wisdom from which the voice of knowing emerges, including the Supreme Teacher, or the Supreme Poet from whom all Love and Knowledge follow.

I understand that aching reach of John Coltrane's horn as he called out "a love supreme, a love supreme," when he sang praise into forever, as a performer in the omnipotent wake of the Supreme Music Maker. Even when we just stand in the presence of our teachers, we are taught.

◆　◆　◆　◆　◆

I AM OBSESSED WITH MAPS and directions. The key to my internal map appears to read something like this:

East: A healer learns through wounding, illness, and death.
North: A dreamer learns though deception, loss, and addiction.

West: A musician learns through silence, loneliness, and
    endless roaming.
South: A poet learns through injustice, wordlessness, and not
    being heard.
Center: A wanderer learns through standing still.

◆ ◆ ◆ ◆ ◆

I STRAINED TO HOLD ON to the back of my father's jean pock-
ets to keep him off my mother. This was my first act of justice. It
was not clean cut. I loved my father as much as I loved my mother.
I still hear the echo as her head slams against the tile bathroom
wall, as he shakes her in a rage that began long before their marriage and at its root has nothing to do with her.

Where within me do I continue to hold that contradiction?

What do I do with this overwhelming need for justice in my
family, for my tribal nation, for those of us in this country who
have been written out of the story or those of us who appear to be
destroyed or perverted by false story?

I've learned there are many genealogies. Within our family is
a genealogy of rage. There is also a genealogy of justice. I would
show you the map, but I am still searching the roadway for casu-
alties. Maybe I can save them. I do not know when rage will end,
or how justice will find its resting place.

I do not want to be haunted by that which I cannot speak.
Or by that which is by nature unspeakable. The truth will not be
uncovered soon enough, cried a mother when her baby was shot
holding a pretend gun in his baby hand while he was playing in the
park, by a man who was believed he was given dominion over all
of the earth because of the color of his skin, because of how much
money he had in the bank, or because of his religion.

Then speak.
Grow poetry in the debris left behind by rage.
Plant so there is enough for everyone to eat.
Make sure there is room for everyone at the table.
Let all of us inhabit the story, in peace.

◆　◆　◆　◆　◆

I HAD A SISTER-IN-LAW WITH whom my mother could speak her deepest truths, because they grew up in the same poverty, the same violence, the same weave of Native with European roots. My mother didn't feel judged by her the way she judged herself for not having a full education, or money. From her, I learned more about my mother's experience of me than from my mother. Through my sister-in-law's revelations I saw my mother observe me as my father's daughter, standing above her and judging her for being lower class, for her lack of education, her poverty.

She told me many things. This sister-in-law told me that my mother depended on me, even when I was small.

"She said you always gave good advice."

This I have kept in my heart, where the maps to make it to a safe home live.

We learned in the months before my mother's death that she was on the drug Thorazine, a drug used in mental institutions for schizophrenia or manic depression, one that left most users with an inability to function. We discovered she was on the drug when she was refused admission to a rehabilitation center, during the last year of her life. With probing we discovered she'd been on it since we were children. The drug had been her companion most of her life. It had seen her through two rough marriages, through hours that added to years of standing on her feet and cooking to provide a living. That she was able to get up and work so many jobs, to continue under its influence, proves her tremendous stamina, which also translates to a stubbornness unmatched only by her granddaughters, and, some would say, me.

I wonder at physicians and a medical system that would keep anyone, especially a physically and mentally healthy woman, on such a powerful antipsychotic. She raised four children, essentially by herself; she worked several jobs, waitressing and cooking, and moved about the world with a dynamism that belied mental instability. What were they attempting to kill in her? Did she say no when she was supposed to say yes?

We took her off the drug without telling her. She never mentioned it, but knowing my mother she must have known, though at that point in her treatment, the morphine stepped in to fill the place that Thorazine had carved out for her to handle life. Every drug has a spirit. It has roots. And like any living thing, it craves life and will search for a way to live.

Without the Thorazine, we got our mother back those last few months of her life. She was more interactive with us. There was a give and take. She was present for her dying and walked through the next door with clarity.

◆ ◆ ◆ ◆ ◆

I HAVE A MEMORY I could never quite place. I am standing under a tree, near brick buildings. The children and I have been driven somewhere far away. Light winds sweep the grassy lawn of the institution and our mother's skirt flutters. How I missed my mother. I almost cannot speak because it hurts. I cling to a stuffed black cat, though I am probably too old to be carrying a stuffed animal with me. I want to know, when is she coming home? Though she is standing close her voice sounds far, far away. She has a cut on her neck that I ask her about, but she does not really answer. The baby toddles off and someone I don't remember brings her back from the gravel driveway near the tree. I keep looking for the mother of sunlight in the kitchen dancing across the polished floor. I cannot find her. The children and I are herded to leave, and when I realize that we have to leave without her, I panic. "No," I cry. "I want my mother." I am quickly placed in the car and the door is slammed tightly behind me. As I write, I remember that someone's hand gets caught in the door. Was it mine? We leave my mother there on the grassy lawn.

I have questioned my brothers and sister, but they don't remember, they were too young. I do not know who brought us to that town to see our mother, nor do I know who took care of us all that time she was gone from us.

I imagine that time is the beginning of the Thorazine.

It wasn't until a few months after our mother's death, when my sister had sifted through old boxes of paperwork, that she found commitment papers for the Eastern State Hospital, an asylum in Vinita, a town a few hours away. We knew nothing of this. We do not know who committed her or why she was committed. I wish my mother had told us this story. What I imagine is that the burden of my father's infidelities broke her, or she had postpartum depression after our youngest brother's birth. He was born in chaos. Nothing was holding. I held on by my fingernails, of which there were none, because during those years I used to bite them to the quick. I would like to tell my mother that I see her story as a story of bravery, of how she found the strength to keep going and find her way out of there. I am evidence of that strength; because of her, I am.

◆　◆　◆　◆　◆

I DO NOT REMEMBER WHEN I first became aware of the presence of my great-grandfather, Henry Marsey Harjo, from Eufaula-Canadian Tribal Town and Wind Clan, except that he was just there and has been looking after me since childhood. He helped me find the way as I have been lost many times. I always come back to stand on the same islands of loss in family, tribal, and earth history. I return to memories of fracture, as if all the broken pieces have voices, and they call me back to witness. They are in need of something I have not been able to give them. They want to be heard. They want to speak.

When I speak, when I create, I am afraid of failing my art, my people, my family. I cannot render with the delicacy, fierceness, and tough beauty in which I perceive. I have failed many times what was given to me to do. I call out, as I have many times before in these moments:

Why did you give me this legacy of poetry, this music, this body, this place from which to speak when I don't look and act the part, and am not the best representative of my people or anyone else, and you made me a woman, when women's voices and worth are not regarded in this society in which we are now living?

That's when I hear and feel my great-grandfather standing near me. He lived a life of integrity and gave all that he had with a great love for his people. He was a Baptist minister. He helped start the Murrow Indian Children's Home, a home for Indian orphans, and he began a mission near Stuart, Florida, for the Seminole people. He was a superintendent for Wealaka Mis-

Joy Harjo

sion, an Indian school in Indian Territory. He was also appointed postal superintendent of the community of Wealaka. He sat in the House of Warriors in tribal government and was appointed by President Herbert Hoover to hold the office of principal *chief* during an interim election. I have uncovered many records of proceedings in which he stood as a moral witness for many disputes and transactions.

My great-grandfather was born just after removal when our people were reestablishing themselves in these new lands. It was a Wild West atmosphere full of drifters, grifters, preachers, and other refugees, all looking for a home in the place where we had been promised by the U.S. government that we'd be free of the settlers who took our homes and pushed us west.

After our people started to reconstruct our lives here, to heal in what became known as Indian Territory, the Civil War broke out, killing even more to add to the losses from that trail of death, and resulted in more theft of land in retribution. Railroads pushed through, taking even more land. The Allotment Act was passed to steal what was left by illegally maneuvering with laws, murders, and any other method of theft. Then oil was discovered. My great-grandfather profited from the discovery of oil on his allotted lands. Most of his and my great-grandmother's allotted lands were in the Henryetta and Eufaula areas, but they also had lands assigned near Kiefer, in the largest oil pool in the world. My great-grandfather had the first car in Okmulgee.

Our people had to negotiate a changing world that did not consider Mvskoke tribal cultural power structures that had served us well for generations. In our society there was no hierarchy of human value based on skin color. We did not decide tribal membership on race or blood quantum. There were no jails, no strangers. We had one of the first liberal immigration policies. We understood and respected plant and animal intelligence. Everyone had a place and not one was above the other. This inherent cultural perspective changed drastically with colonial influence.

My great-grandfather really doesn't have to say much with words. Just his presence often tells me what I need to remember. Though he was born around 1860 and passed from this world when he was seventy-one years of age, time means nothing in the place we inhabit together. We speak without the burden of words. This is where I see him, find him, in the heart territory between us. I know the quality of love he carried, and the burden.

He listens to me complain about failures.

Yes, I know failure, he nods. *I can't tell you about being a woman*, he says, *but God loves all of his creations. Not one is above the other. Let's sit together and listen. Then we will pray for a path that will lift up the people, all people, including all the beloved beings of creation. You will find yourself in that lifting up.*

I have some of my great-grandfather's handwriting on lined paper from his sermon preparations. His handwriting was thoughtful, even, and tells of a man who writes with a great tenderness for the gift of life. It tells me that he was a seeker, and he loved his people. The church provided an architecture for the deep spiritual awareness that is inherent in our Muscogee Creek people. They love their church and their hymn singing, which is a mix of Mvskoke and Judeo-Christian forms. They love their lands, their culture, their ceremonies. They made the church their ceremonial grounds as they structured their worship around our original rituals and practices.

These memories, and the stories in these words, might appear to exist in the long ago. In the short-root mind, a kind of mind of a people whose children don't even know the names of their great-grandparents, there is no past. Everything is right now. This kind

My great-grandmother Katie Monahwee, great-grandfather Henry Marsey Harjo, (might be) Billy Bowlegs, and unidentified Seminole man in Fort Pierce, Florida

of mind has its roots in the material culture, in what can be accumulated. My great-grandfather reminds me that we need to keep within the long-rooted mind. Because of the longer roots we have a larger structure of knowing from which to take on understanding.

❖   ❖   ❖   ❖   ❖

HOW LOVE BLOWS THROUGH THE TREES

This old Creek town appears empty except for the trees
And the story of how wind will come to clean
The earth, of the takers who took

And never give back.
One day, my grandfather used to sing
A fresh world will rise up
To take the place of a society
That didn't love the earth.

We lost ourselves when we crossed the river
My grandfather used to say
He would smoke to the east, north, west, and south
And touch the earth and the sky
To bless.
He'd be standing in the kitchen
And there'd be no one listening.

Pass this love on, he'd say.
It knows how to bend and will never break.
It's the only thing with a give and take,
The more it's used the more it makes.

My grandfather flew like smoke to the sky side of earth.
He left us here in this place he blessed.
What stories he carried, what laughter wrapped memory:
Of a people who never knew themselves
As strangers in these lands.
Now I'm standing in the kitchen
And I can hear him singing,
Sometimes it takes a while for us to hear.

Pass this love on, he'd say.
It knows how to bend and will never break.

Joy Harjo

It's the only thing with a give and take,
The more it's used the more it makes.

That love is the bridge that will cross the river home.
He'd be standing in the dark with no one listening.
How time blows steadily through the city, the trees.
Sing to this earth, sing, he sang.

◆ ◆ ◆ ◆ ◆

MY MOTHER TOOK US TO a Methodist church very early in my life. We did not go regularly, especially in the summer when our weekends often found us at one of the many lakes surrounding the Tulsa area. When she began working outside our home, she was so tired from working full-time, caring for four children, and being a full-time homemaker that any regular churchgoing stopped.

One afternoon a local evangelical church sent flyers advertising vacation bible school with suckers attached and passed them out as I stood on the steps of the elementary school waiting for my neighbor friends to walk home together. I began attending because of the candy. We did handicrafts, like decorating a clock on small wood planks printed with "God's Time." I liked the singing and there were cookies. I liked the stories as many of them spoke to a spiritual living. I did not like the threats that I would burn in fires of hell if I did not accept their way as the only way.

I liked to think without words about the meaning of life. When I was outside alone in the early morning hours, I learned to think spiritually. The trees, the earth, the sky, all the insects and creatures shined as exactly who they were. They did not have to concern themselves with burning in hell. They just were, and in their world, I felt a kind of peace that was nowhere else, not in the house, nor in the church. I knew who I was there in that world peopled by elements, plants, and animals, and I was not afraid.

There were many in that evangelical church who took me in, who were kind people. However, in church, as in most social organizations, there were strict rules about who belonged and who didn't belong. Because my parents were "non-believers" and did not attend our church, they would go to hell. I was given excellent instruction on hell every Sunday morning and evening and Wednesday night. Hell was terrible with fire, and according to the preacher, it was filled with everyone in the world who did not belong to our church or other churches like it. The description of heaven was not appealing either, with its streets of gold and believers in robes playing harps. People who happened to be born in Korea, Africa, or other "heathen" countries, or who danced at the ceremonial grounds, were destined for hell if they didn't have the word of God. Even your own mother and father would go to hell if you did not bring them to the altar.

When I washed my mother's back every evening when she got off work, as she smoked and drank her Royal Crown Cola in the sudsy tub, I would preach to her about hell. My mother always responded to my entreaties that she was raised a Methodist and believed in God. And where were her cigarettes? She didn't need to go to their church.

If I took those stories and thoughts of hell and placed them in the crook of the tree in our yard, then the tree helped relieve the wheel of worry that followed the questions that turned in me. Why would the Creator-God make everything, then deem only those who were of a certain religion or church worthy of an eternal life? If we were made in the likeness of our Creator, then doesn't that mean everyone? The church reminded me of those social clubs in school that I would never be part of because my parents divorced, we were Indian, our house wasn't kept up to the standard of everyone else's home in the neighborhood, and my mother worked.

If my mother wasn't in heaven, I wasn't going there either.

◆　◆　◆　◆　◆

I LOVED THE PSALMS IN the Bible. They were essentially poems, written by tribal people much like my Mvskoke people. This is where I found one of the poems I still love most, Psalm 23, from the King James Version of the Bible:

> The LORD is my shepherd; I shall not want.
> He maketh me to lie down in green pastures: he leadeth
> 　　me beside the still waters.
> He restoreth my soul: he leadeth me in the paths
> 　　of righteousness for his name's sake.
> Yea, though I walk through the valley of the shadow
> 　　of death, I will fear no evil: for thou art with
> 　　me; thy rod and thy staff they comfort me.
> Thou preparest a table before me in the
> 　　presence of mine enemies: thou anointest
> 　　my head with oil; my cup runneth over.
> Surely goodness and mercy shall follow me
> 　　all the days of my life: and I will dwell
> 　　in the house of the LORD for ever.

The psalm, "The Lord Is My Shepherd," came from other tribal communities, far across oceans and deserts. Poetry could travel, just like birds or airplanes. It was a prayer poem of protection. It was most likely accompanied by music. The rhythm quickens and I imagine a leader who loves me, my mother or father, or my great-grandfather walking with me along one of the many rivers here, or alongside one of the lakes we visited on the weekends. The table set before me was filled with plates of fried chicken, bowls of mashed potatoes and cream gravy. There were green beans, fried bread, fresh tomatoes, and pies of every kind of your favorite: cherry, peach, or apple. And cold watermelon cut into slices that you would take out to the porch to eat, and for seed-spitting contests.

The rod and the staff were like my father's bow he used for deer hunting. In the poem he was protecting me. The poem-song was both a prayer of protection for my father and me, and a prayer to protect me from him. This was another paradox. I felt my father's paradox of living, without speaking it or having words for it. I knew it within the place of knowing which is often without words.

The shadow of death is my little dog Alligator's body laid out on the driveway after being hit by one of the cars he tried to catch, the car he finally did. It is my father disappearing into the night, to find or make trouble.

I didn't know what "righteous" meant but I liked the sound. Eventually I would own a dictionary and look up what I did not know.

I came to know that poem by heart, because I was given little prizes in church for memorizing, like glow-in-the-dark crosses of Jesus hanging by his nailed hands. To memorize was the only way I could go to church camp because we did not have money to go. We could pick what we recited. I learned this psalm.

The Twenty-third Psalm is a poem from people who knew the earth. From people who, much like the Navajo, tend sheep and in

Joy Harjo

doing so learn respect for the plants, animals, and elements with whom we live.

There is no one way to God, no one correct spiritual path, no one way to write poetry. There is no one roadway, no one-way Bering Strait, no one kind of flowering plant, no one kind of tiger, no one way to knowledge. Diversity characterizes this planet, this galaxy, this universe.

In that church, a story about Noah and his sons was turned into a moral tale on why dark-skinned people were not worthy of the respect and care afforded to light-skinned people—

That is why I left.

◆　◆　◆　◆　◆

WHEN I WAS YOUNG, I killed a bird with my hands. I loved animals, and the backyard was my refuge because the house often didn't feel safe. I would go out into that yard of mostly grass, low bushes, and vines of poison ivy that crawled up the backside of the house, and there I would find all kinds of playmates with whom to share life. I would find garter snakes, June bugs, and earthworms, and every now and then, a box turtle would venture through and delight us.

I don't recall the upset of that day. It usually had to do with my father. He was spending most evenings after work away from home. He had movie star looks and moved like a well-groomed cat through the streets and the bars, in the sleek cars bought with his Indian oil money checks. Even when he was home, he was passing through. All the women he met as he disappeared into the dark wanted to take him into their arms and mother him. They constantly vied for his attention, even with my mother, his wife, on his arm. He would always look and touch. It made for an unspoken insecurity in all of us, his children and his wife.

That day of the killing was no different than any other. If there was a fight, it was always the same. They were about my father's women, and his drinking. Those two bad habits were neck and neck in a contest, and neither would win. My father had a good work ethic and sweated in an airline hangar repairing engines for American Airlines, headquartered in Tulsa. His job made the down payment on our small white house with red painted shutters, bought clothes and groceries. The house enabled my mother to unfold the chest of her dreams which included being a singer, a songwriter, and a mother of four children. A few years into the dream, everything was broken, no matter her efforts to hold everything together with love songs.

We were nearing the irreparable break line that early evening I wandered into the backyard alone. It was dusk, that liminal time in which dark and light brush up against each other. Even if my parents weren't fighting yet, I could feel the tension between them snapping with the weight of heartbreak. Once it started, he would hurt her, then look for us. For her to leave would open the door to the deep untouchable grief of his mother's death. For him to leave would mean the death of all my mother had fought for as she walked away from the shame of poverty.

As I write this, I realize that I am just like my brother who is eighteen months younger than me, whose stories are often crowded with abandonment by our parents. I tell him to get over it, because a replay of the story that will always trap us makes a muddy, ugly rut. But here I am with him, one of the little children stumbling behind our parents as our father rages and fights, begging him to stop.

I felt the bird thinking before I saw him. Communication with

Joy Harjo

birds, animals, and plants is intuitive, without words. The robin stood on the steel pole of the metal fence that made a line between the neighbor's yard and ours, looking over at me. I felt a premonition. I'm not sure how to explain it, but I knew I was coming into a test. And I had a sense I was going to fail. The robin had a similar sense of fate, and that knowing linked us.

The sun had gone down below the horizon and no one had called me in. I felt uncared for. I looked over for the robin and he'd hopped off the fence line and was now closer to me. Maybe I could catch him. Why would I want to do that? There was no reason, only a churning of fears and insecurities. I was too often sick. My stomach hurt too much. My throat hurt. I was in the way. I was a burden. I was angry but I buried it so it would not destroy me. I have a hard time owning anger even now.

Without thinking, I began to stalk the robin. I didn't know why. Robin flew up out of my way, and then touched down again. I had always been friends with the robins, with all the animals. There had been no reason to suspect me of such behavior, thought the robin. I jumped and the robin landed on the wire fence. Fury overtook me, and with sudden effort I landed on the robin, smothering him under me, clutching the bird in my hands, close to my heart.

For years I have replayed this moment of my shame. I can still feel the robin's beating heart slow to a stop in my hands. I feel the limp release of death. I had killed a creature who I had long admired, from anger, the bird with the beautiful scarlet feathered breast, and songs that I knew from the beginning of my knowing in that house. I knew better. I broke the law.

Even when we are young, we know things. We know when we have broken a law. We don't always know how to put things back together.

◆ ◆ ◆ ◆ ◆

YEARS LATER WHEN I RETURNED to Oklahoma, I bought my sister's home in Glenpool because she inherited our mother's home in Tulsa. I knew the robin family there. I met many generations because my sister's family lived there nearly forty years. As I moved in, the robin elder watched me. He had questions. I told him who I was, and that I was living there now. He was satisfied with that and went peacefully about his business. Then I began going out every morning for prayers and often took one of my flutes. He and the other birds had quite a discussion among themselves about it. They decided that I was a strange and rare hybrid of human and bird.

When I left that house to move in with my husband, to his home in Tulsa, I missed that robin and his family terribly. One morning when the missing was especially acute, I opened the front door to step out into the new day, and there on the lawn was a contingent of over fifty robins to greet me!

Part Two

BECOMING

◆ ◆ ◆ ◆ ◆

Girl-Warrior was becoming
a woman.
One day she was the sun,
Another she was the moon.
One day she hated everyone.
The next day she was so overcome
With beauty she could not stand it.
She cried out to the Old Ones
Who had promised her they would be there
When she called.
Where were they, she demanded
To no one there.

They waited until she was dreaming.
It was only then that she could hear them,
Because the electronic frequencies of stereo,
Television, and radio signals interfered
As they zigzagged
The wave of civilization.

She dreamed of the path from the stars—
How it shimmered with geometric
Forms and colors that gave nourishment
And impetus for beauty.
She dreamed of boys.

Because she had no coming-of-age ceremony
They gave her one in spirit.
This was her ceremony song:

The Life of Beauty

The sung blessing of creation
Led her into the human story.
That was the first beauty.

Next beauty was the sound of her mother's voice
Rippling the waters beneath the drumming skin
Of her birthing cocoon.

Next beauty the father with kindness in his hands
As he held the newborn against his breathing.

Next beauty the moon through the dark window,
It was a rocking horse, a wish.

There were many beauties in this age
For everything was immensely itself:
Green greener than the impossibility of green,
the taste of wind after its slide through dew grass at dawn,
Or language running through a tangle of wordlessness in
     her mouth.

She ate well of the next beauty.

Next beauty planted itself urgently beneath the warrior shrines.

Next was beauty beaded by her mother and pinned neatly
To hold back her hair.

Then how tendrils of fire longing grew into her,

Beautiful the flower
Between her legs as she became herself.

Do not forget this beauty she was told.

The story took her far away from beauty. In the tests
  of her living,
Beauty was often long from the reach of her mind and spirit.
When she forgot beauty, all was brutal.
But beauty always came to lift her up to stand again.

When it was beautiful all around and within,
She knew herself to be corn plant, moon, and sunrise.

Death is beautiful, she sang, as she left this story behind her.

Even her bones, said time
Were tuned to beauty.

❖   ❖   ❖   ❖   ❖

I WAS LIKE MOST DAUGHTERS ducking or prancing through the doorway of adolescence. I could do it better. I was invincible. I was smarter than my mother. And like any braggart, I was destined to stumble.

I made the decision that I would be different; I would make my own life, free of marriage, of violence and the dominance of the belief system that demands that women must have a husband and children to be happy. I had not seen that happiness in my home, or in many of the homes around me. Instead, I saw an unattainable realm of romantic dreams in a perfect sky that never rained, and the roadway of hard reality on which ordinary human life prevailed. Desire ran the track between them. It was the fast, red speedster that raced the edge of disaster. Only one person could fit in that car, at the most, two. It does not hold a family.

I wanted to be an artist, free to create without the weight of societal expectation to doom me. I thrilled that my body was changing, that I had begun the road to selfhood. I created art that won awards, I was the family trickster always trying to make everyone laugh with the cartoons I'd draw, the stunts, the plays I'd construct of family drama. Yet, I was constantly terrified, and my life felt in danger.

Because of my burgeoning womanliness I had to run from neighborhood men who saw that I had no one protecting me. They smelled my vulnerability. I had no father guarding the door to protect me. The boys who used to be my playmates teased and tried to get a touch. I couldn't sleep for the monsters looking in the window, hiding under the bed, sitting on my chest. I couldn't sleep because I was trying to keep away from the monster now married to my mother who was snoring in the next room, who came too close when my mother was at work and we were home alone. I would finally fall to sleep when I would hear my mother's alarm for work at five in the morning.

Unlike the childhood fairy tales that I read alone, there would be no one to save me. My mother and I were lost in the same fairy tale. She was supposed to marry a prince or a king, but instead, she married the monster and took her children with her.

When I hit puberty, I was locked to the destiny of my physical body. There was no more flying and dreaming in eternal time, there was only here and survival. There was a fire burning in my body, the same dangerous desire that had led my mother to disaster. I did not know how to put it out, nor did I want to—the flickering and burning made me crazy with unrest. I wanted to write, paint, sing, and play music but I lacked confidence or encouragement or even a place in which to safely practice.

I needed a safe room. I needed a story. I was shedding my childhood body, like a snake shedding its skin, or like the breaking of the chrysalis woven by the worm to reveal flight. I did not know how to let go, nor did I understand fully how to occupy my becoming self. One day I was water. The next day I had become fire.

I stayed lost within my room. I read ponderous novels by Dickens; I read Shakespeare or Louisa May Alcott. I bought records from a popular record club. They'd come in the mail once a month. I looked forward to the ritual of opening up the cardboard around those lifesaver discs, reading the liner notes, taking in the cover art, and then carefully laying the platter on the record player, lifting up the needle, and placing it in the groove. I danced to James Brown. I listened to the Yardbirds, Ray Charles, Cream, and Jefferson Airplane. Then Janis Joplin came along. Aretha Franklin was a goddess in the pantheon. I would come in after school then go into the room I shared with my sister. I reveled in the short crevice of time to listen and sing along, before he came in from work. Then one day, the monster came home early to find me singing in my room and because I was happy, he forbade me to sing in the house, his house.

I wanted to save my mother, but I was bound. I was learning that you cannot save anyone unless they want to be saved. You could lose everything, even yourself, in your failed efforts.

I became the best boxer in the neighborhood when I boxed with my brother and his friends in one of his friends' garages down the street. I wanted my own gloves, but because I was a girl my mother refused to buy them for me, and she would not allow me to buy them with money I earned. I got my first bra. I was named an understudy in an operetta. I drew and drew images that would protect me.

I was alone in my ceremony of becoming. We had no circle of extended family. Everyone had been excommunicated by the monster. No one could come near us, not even friends. They were afraid of him.

The monster found my diary. He broke the lock to open it. He read my stupid lines. He read my stupid poetry. He read of my stupid junior high crushes to everyone in the family, in a mocking voice.

If he could find a diary kept hidden in the most secret place, I was not safe. But I had never been safe. Just a few weeks before the diary incident he made my mother play Russian roulette in front of my brothers and sister, when I was gone, when I couldn't be there to fight and protect her.

There is no place else to go with such a story. In the fairy tale of the American Dream no one will believe Native children over a white stepfather. In all the stories we watched in the movies and on television, the Native, Black, and Asian characters were first to be killed, to die.

❖   ❖   ❖   ❖   ❖

I AM FIFTEEN YEARS OLD. I have no father god to protect me. Neither does my sister nor do my brothers. My sister and I have divided our room into sides. I drew an invisible line down the center of the bed. I was not always kind, and in moments when I clean my internal house of memories I go back and change my behavior in situations that haunt me for my unkind acts. And continue forward in the best manner possible.

My sister is a good soul. Our mother crowned her "perfect,"

which set her against the rest of us, my brothers and I who were prone to inventiveness and misbehavior. I understand now, with time as the ruler of my house of memory, that my mother appreciated her quiet manner, how she walked along, and probably very alone, a path that would bring my mother the most peace in that place in time we found ourselves in together. She witnessed my fight, my stands for justice that never ended well as I often found myself at the end of our stepfather's belt. And my sister saw how easily that belt would be pulled out because of his frustration at work, the pressure of exerting jealous control over our beautiful mother, and irritation at having four "mongrel" (his word) children in his house whom he did not want. My sister was stealthy, especially after her first and last beating when we moved from our childhood home into a home my mother decided to make with him.

I was the usual target. I looked and moved like my Native father and his family. I told the truth and spoke up. I had been my mother's protector but soon learned she did not want my protection against her new husband. She was punished by him for going against him when she stood with me or any of the other children.

We all have ties, or cords, with each other, with memories and places. Some share good thoughts back and forth. There is a healthy give and take. Others are parasitical in nature. They can be used to suck energy or harm you. Some can be used as paths for prayer to assist. Some are by relatives, by people you know, even those who have gone on and cannot let go. Others are by those you don't know at all.

Once I felt someone send a cord in, even saw it looking about to attach itself. I did not like the feeling of it but because I was blinded with "falling in love," I let it. I wanted intimacy. But I came to learn the cord was more about staking claim, for control. I had to find it and cut it.

I feel a thick cord. It connects my spirit to a memory that I have tried to forget. I have pretended it wasn't there, and I drank or even smoked my way around it when I was younger. Then I buried the memory under accomplishment. My story is stalled here, as if the cord has choked off the rest of the story and I cannot move forward. As the story maker, I have to find a way. First, I need to speak and remember what I do not want to remember. Even now, years later, when my mother is gone, even the monster is gone, I have come to understand they do not want the haunting either. They want to move on.

I remember the stacked laundry basket by my bed. I was in charge of washing, drying, and ironing the clothes. The clothes that needed to be ironed were on my side of the room. I remember the thin yellow light from the low-wattage bulb in the overhead lamp and the cheap wallpaper. My mother had been in the living room ironing my stepfather a shirt. She ironed his clothes. I ironed the rest, including her uniforms for work.

My stepfather was in his chair in the living room as she ironed. He sat there and gave out orders. My mother called at me to come in there. I did not want to go in there because I was wearing something for bed that had come in a giveaway box. It was of a very thin fabric. I quickly looked about for something to cover me.

He yelled out for me to listen to my mother and get in there right away or he was getting his belt. All of the laundry was now on the floor from my desperate search, but his demand told me that I had better get in there, no matter how I was dressed, or I would be beaten. I slinked into the living room, my arms snug over my chest, to do my mother's bidding. I left as quickly as possible, back to my room.

My mother followed me to the door of my room. I had never seen her bristling with such anger toward me. She told me that if

Joy Harjo

I ever paraded in front of her husband like that again, she would throw me out of the house, onto the street. Then she walked away, back to him.

That's when my spirit walked away from her and his house. I was not interested in her man; I was doing my best to keep out of the reach of his hands when she wasn't around. She had never spoken to me in that manner. She abandoned me with her words, and I began to look for a way out.

The injustice of it all felt unbearable. We would keep living with the monster, and now, my mother was on his side. Beer or cheap vodka knocked out my pain, or rather, slid the knowledge of it beneath the consciousness where it could not keep hurting me. I had never felt so alone. The hurt led me down paths where I gave myself away for nothing.

But at this moment, years later, here I am with the cord in my hands. In the last months of my mother's life, as I helped care for her, I thought I had let it all go.

I thank the story for what it is teaching me, I cut the cord. It shrivels. I feed it to the fire. The story turns to ashes. The ashes return to earth. My mother, my children, my grandchildren, and I are now free.

◆　◆　◆　◆　◆

Girl-Warrior lied and said she was going out with her friend
To hang out at her house.
She wasn't a friend, rather a girl she barely knew
And had a bad feeling when she asked her to double-date.
Girl-Warrior was not allowed to date.
Nor was she usually allowed to go anywhere with friends
Or without.

But she begged her mother.
And her stepfather was working late, i.e., he was seeing
A woman on the other side of town.
Girl-Warrior got in the car and knew her fate was in the hands
Of reckless strangers.
She had a dime taped inside her shoe for a phone call,
But who would she call if there was trouble?
No one.
They drove to another town.
Her "date" was ten years older. He bought them beer.
What the hell.
It was the first time she had anything resembling a date.
She wanted to be normal.
Every drink made her feel more and more
Normal.
Girl-Warrior's new girlfriend left with her boyfriend
Without telling her.
She saw the red of their taillights disappear
Into a darkness
That grew larger and larger
Until Girl-Warrior had no way to get home.
She just wanted to be normal.
Drink Cokes, flip her hair back and laugh
With someone who might offer his hand,
His jacket, or other small kindness between new friends.
There was more beer.
If she wanted a ride before her stepfather
Made it back to the house, she had to pay
The darkness
Either way.

Joy Harjo

THIS IS HOW I CAME of age, by a tightrope slung between my desires and the desires of others. I was hungry for ritual. Ritual creates belonging. We are all in a ritual marked by sunrise, daylight, sunset, night, and moon phases. We also move within the ritual of the changing of seasons, either fall, winter, spring, and summer, or dry and rainy seasons. Our cultural practices are arranged according to these earth rituals.

We all need rituals of becoming, in which we are given instructions that define our relationship with becoming, with our relatives, those sharing the whole world around us. This is how it was meant to be, for those coming up, at all stages of our becoming in this life. In these times, however, of degradation of our physical, mental, and spiritual sources of nourishment, we are losing ourselves and our children. Until we understand and act as if we are the earth, then each of us will experience the pain of separation from sacred knowledge, from ourselves.

I walk back in time to help make a coming-of-age ceremony for Girl-Warrior. I construct a doorway where sunrise is a line above a dark blue horizon. Her grandmothers and great-grandmothers gather around and speak. The ancestors appear here to help because she is one of us. She is us. She is worthy of love, of tenderness, of all that she needs to create a future. The world lives within the cradle of her hips. She is every girl, this girl.

They tell her that every seven years marks a renewal, a shift, and a test. Seven is considered a sacred number. Within it are the four directions, above, below, and within. It makes a complete cycle.

They tell her that the second cycle of seven in our lives marks a crisis in becoming. We mature into adulthood. A boy becomes a man. A girl becomes a woman. Becoming includes a countless range of gender expression.

"Be exactly who you are," they tell her, "in your becoming."

They remind her she is holding tremendous power, and power has two sides. It can harm or heal.

To hold such power can be difficult; that's why we need guidance in ritual and ceremony, especially at this age, but at any age, for power without grounding and sharing can destroy.

In our Mvskoke tribal traditions, adolescence is a time of teaching and celebration, the Old Ones say.

"As you enter this doorway of womanhood," they tell her, "you must keep the fire going of *vkvsvmkv*, or spiritual belief. You must seek and acquire a spiritual understanding of life. Your relationship with your Creator is central. You must tend it with quiet and communion. Turn your eyes and ears inward and listen. Begin every morning, tending this fire.

"*Emetvl'hvmke* is community. Your body is a community of organs, all living with consciousness, that work together to house you in this story. Community is those with whom you live, from home to school, to your tribal nation, city, or state. You must remember to place community interest and benefits ahead of individual and personal gain.

"Always be kind and humble. *Eyasketv* is humility. No one is above the other.

"*Vrakkueckv* means respect. Respect this gift of life, and in doing so we respect ourselves and others.

"*Fvccetv* is integrity. Be honest. Tell the truth. Keep an ethical stance. If you sense that someone calling themself "friend" is not your friend, then be honest with yourself and act accordingly.

"*Emenhonretv tayat* translates as trust. Take responsibility for every act, thought, or dream.

Joy Harjo

"*Hoporrenkv* is the continual gaining of wisdom. Listen. Study hard, beloved granddaughter.

"*En'homahtetv* is leadership. We are all put here to be leaders, within ourselves, our families, and our communities. Be a leader.

"Do not forget that we are here and will always be here for you. You can call on us at any time. We love you."

They wrap Girl-Warrior in a new blanket and walk her out through the doorway of her beginning, which is also a new beginning for us, her family. A beautiful sunrise brightens the sky. They give her a new name. She is given gifts. One gives her plants that will help her help herself and others. Another reminds her of the ability to dream stories to be shared. She is given a pen and paper. She is given words. Another gives her back the music that was stolen from her by the monster. She is given a song that will keep her to the right direction. You are becoming in a time in which you will see the world turn upside down before it is renewed, they tell her.

◆　◆　◆　◆　◆

When Girl-Warrior stepped from the circle of ceremony
Into the new day, she was transformed.
She was now a woman.
The Old Ones had given her a woman's name.
She would now be called "Poet Warrior"
To assist in making her path on this earth
In times that would need what poetry
Could bring, for knowledge,
Compassion, and healing
And could be used as a tool for digging and defense
To unearth the truth, when needed.

Poet Warrior stretched, then pulled on her jeans.
She washed her face with water, which she was told
By the Old Ones, washed the dreaming state
From the night away,
So that she could engage fully
In the realm ruled by the sun.
She remembered to go out into the morning
And give thanks, as they had reminded her.
She ate some toast with apple jam, hoisted on her school bag
And went to classes.

◆　◆　◆　◆　◆

CHILDREN COMING OF AGE NEED to be taught by the elders who pass on what has strengthened and inspired them in life. When this time of becoming is honored by their families, their community, the young ones emerge into adulthood with the lit charge to develop spiritually, mentally, and physically, and are an intimate part of carrying the community into the future. They are empowered by being brought through the doorway in celebration.

◆　◆　◆　◆　◆

ONE OF MY FAVORITE GIRL-BECOMING stories I learned when I visited a tribal nation in the Pacific Northwest. I was told how when a family member had reached the time of becoming, she was taken into the longhouse. She was taught by her relatives, the women in the community. She was given a time to fast, to get to know herself and understand the teachings. This time allowed for the teachings to plant themselves deeply into the mind, body, and spiritual memory. One young relative was given a song by the

Joy Harjo

ancestors in her dreaming. When she was brought into the circle after her fasting to share, she sang the song. The Old Ones recognized the song with tears of joy. This song had belonged to a great-grandmother, a relative who had long passed before she was born, and it had now returned to the family, to the people, by this young woman's efforts. To know that she was surrounded with such love in a circle that extended beyond death strengthened the young woman. She would use that knowledge throughout her life. The ceremony strengthened the family, the whole community.

I visited this community when I was in high school, part of one of the first all-Native drama and dance troupes. I am still in touch with the people there and feel great affection for them. They remember the time we went and visited them.

◆ ◆ ◆ ◆ ◆

WHEN MY MOTHER PASSED, I inherited an iron cooking pot brought over on the Trail that belonged to her mother's mother.

Some of the most important stories are not in words, not in poems or other forms of speaking, but in objects of use and beauty. This cooking pot is one of the most potent stories I carry, made at the end of the century before last, one of many such pots used by Native people east of the Mississippi. The one that was passed through generations of women came to me from my mother. It tells of survival, of the labors of women who cooked, cleaned, and uplifted everyone with stories and songs. The pot is sitting by my feet while I am writing. It was pressed with fury and fire. It was made of the same materials as weapons. It made soup and fed those who gathered around it to eat. In hard times soup was water of a few bones and hope. Other times thick and boiling with meat, vegetables, and herbs. It was feast and laughing. It's the same kind of pot we use at the ceremonial grounds for squirrel soup. My mother planted flowers in it. It was my only request from her belongings when she passed. I chose it over any jewelry or furniture. I am planting these memories for my daughters and granddaughters and great-granddaughters, so they will know their worth, so they will be good cooks like the ancestral line of mothers before them. Or most of them. My mother's mother was better kept away from the cooking fire!

◆ ◆ ◆ ◆ ◆

WE NEED TO KEEP UP strong women's councils to work in tandem with the men's circles. We need both female and male to make balanced posts for the doorway of life. Balance is built into our traditional ways of thinking. Just as our men are encouraged to be strong and knowledgeable, so are our women.

We lost some elderly grounds members this year, and at one of our first events of the season we women were washing up the stacks of pans and dishes after cooking, serving, and eating. We were drying them and putting them in stacks according to what belonged to whom as we joked, as we used the water hose now and then to spray everyone, to cool us down, with much delight. There were two stacks of pans for two women who had passed this year, who were no longer with us. We were still using their pans, honoring their place and contributions, as they had honored us with their cooking and presence.

I still use some of my mother's skillets and measuring cups. I like handling them, knowing they were hers, that she used them to sustain us.

◆ ◆ ◆ ◆ ◆

Joy Harjo

Birth of Fire in the Dawn of Time
    Fire leaps from the Sun
    And is caught in the Heart
Time is a Father of Fire. He procreates with Imagination, or Mother
    Fire
Gives birth to universes
    Fire
Universes give birth to other universes
    Fire
There are many universes of becoming
    Fire
Fire was tamed for warmth
    Fire
Was tamed for cooking
    Fire
The sizzle of Deer meat, Rabbit
    Fire
There is a pathway between the Heart and the Sun
    Fire
A good cook honors Fire
    Fire
Her mothers, grandmothers, great-grandmothers,
All the way to Fire
    Fire
My mother was a cook
    Fire
I began cooking at eight
    Fire

I have cooked all of my life
        Fire
My sons, my daughters cook with respect for Fire
        Fire
I have a cooking pot made with elements
From the first Fire
        Fire
I will pass on the cooking pot to generations
Behind me. They are alive with creative fire
        Fire
There are countless generations in the genealogy of Fire
        Fire
Cooking is transformation by fire
        Fire
We are firekeepers
        Fire
We make Fire with Fire
        Fire Fire

◆　◆　◆　◆　◆

When she came home from school
Poet Warrior climbed up her favorite tree
With her notebook of drawings
And words.
Some words she tried then scribbled out.
Others flew into the air as she sang them
Like fury or love.
Others were holders for all the places she wanted to visit.
Words made a path to other worlds
That she could follow without fail or failing.

She followed sounds by drawing and singing them.
She wrote the initials of the boy she liked.
She sang of the mysterious girl who knew poetry
Better than anyone else.
She wrote sadness, grief, and fear like word beads.
She wrote them in code that no one else could break
Unless they knew the tune.
She hid her notebook wrapped in grocery bag paper
In the tree.
She hid in her notebook of unspeakable truths
When there was no place left to hide,
When her stepfather chased off her father
With a loaded gun.

✦ ✦ ✦ ✦ ✦

WHEN I GAVE BIRTH TO my son when I was seventeen, at the old W. W. Hastings Indian Hospital in Tahlequah, I didn't know that just a few miles away in that Cherokee enclave of Moodys, Oklahoma, was where my maternal grandmother had been born to my maternal great-grandmother, Lena Evans. She died in child-birth. Her father, Tom Christian, was left with two small daughters, my grandmother Leona and her sister, Mattie. They were then raised there by a full-blood Cherokee family who my grandmother said used her for labor. My grandmother's sister stayed close to her adoptive family and became a teacher. My mother said that at her aunt's funeral there were only full-blood Cherokee families.

The Cherokee Nation marriage certificate for my great-grandmother Lena Evans states that she was eighteen years old when she married Tom Christian, who was forty-five. I wonder about arranged marriage in 1903. I heard of them happening in our Oklahoma tribal communities. When I was in my very early twenties, I met a young woman from a southern plains tribal nation whose grandfather arranged a marriage with her to an older man. He promised her grandfather to take good care of her and pay for her education. I questioned her about it, as I had never heard of such a thing taking place in my generation. She told me that he was a good man and treated her respectfully. He supported her in getting her degree. She was very happy with him and her life with him.

Most likely my great-grandmother was married off young because her family was poor and without resources. She knew her choices were very limited, even nonexistent.

"They used to call me Cotton-Top," my grandmother told me once when I was so young that words were enlivened beings marching and leaping through my mind. This was the same day I saw my first hummingbird, shimmering in sunlight, as it drank from a red flower. I watched as my grandmother let down her pinned-up hair to brush it out. My mother had dropped us children off to stay with our grandparents for two weeks that summer. Their house smelled of stones, canned peaches, and kerosene. I brushed my grandmother's hair, which extended long past her waist. In that full-blood community she grew up in, my grandmother's light hair marked her. She did not fit.

I imagine my grandmother as a headlong teenager, long-legged and beautiful but misplaced. When a good-looking young man gave her some attention, she walked through the only door possible, to a similar life, a life without pretty things to wear, a life of drudgery and hard labor as she raised six sons and one daughter on nothing but what could be planted and dug from the earth.

By the time I came along the struggle of poverty had exhausted

Joy Harjo

my grandmother. Her breath was ragged with asthma. Her shoes were cut with holes to accommodate bunions. All she had left were her stories.

When I visited with my grandparents, in whatever one- or two-room place they were living as sharecropper tenants, my grandmother followed me around, telling me stories. When I would wake up in the morning, before I touched my feet to the cold, worn linoleum floor after waiting for the live wood ashes in the stove to be urged to flames for heat, she would be telling stories. She would have cooked breakfast at dawn, before everyone was awake, to get to her story making. The eggs and biscuits would be congealed and cold, sitting on the table for us.

She told us to keep away from doors and windows during thunderstorms in order not to attract the lightning. She told unfolding intricate dramas of families in countries she would never have the money to visit. I don't remember the details of her stories, but I dream the same kinds of stories. It was as if the stories needed planting, and I appeared to be the most fertile place for them to continue. Maybe because of her powerful dreams, her storytelling, I can go all the places she dreamed.

The older she got, the more her stories became focused on the deaths of her friends and community members, and on all the ways people meet their deaths. The one she repeated most was of a neighbor man's death in the graveyard just up the road. She took me over there to show me the place. Most of the gravestones were metal placards with plastic clear windows, under which there was a place to slide a card with the departed's information. "One minute," she told me, "he was walking across the graveyard just like us, then the next minute he was dead of a heart attack, right here." She showed me the spot. The gruesome coincidence was pleasing to both of us.

If our grandchildren are evidence of our fulfilled dreams, then our grandparents are the dreamers and storytellers from whose imagination we arrive here. Yet, if I could, I would go back to my grandmother's youth, as she leaped from childhood to womanhood to motherhood. I would give her a table and chair for her use only, paper and a pen or even a typewriter, encouragement and love, and all the time in the world to write her stories.

◆　◆　◆　◆　◆

AFTER MY MOTHER'S DEATH I Googled her full birth name to see what would come up, if anything, in the search. What a surprise when a marriage record appeared, documenting her marriage at age sixteen to a man twice her age in Independence, Kansas. She kept this secret her whole life from her children. I wonder if anyone else knew, including her husbands or even her best friends.

The only clue I had of anything like this comes in the only other story similar in my catalog of mother stories. My mother used to tell us about running away to join the carnival, and how her brothers came looking for her and took her back home.

That was one of my favorite mother stories. I imagined her in a red satin outfit, much like my tap costume, climbing atop a circus elephant. I knew it had been a carnival, not a circus, but my imagination preferred to construct a circus, not the dusty, garish setup of a cheap country carnival that moved weekly from small town to small town, as it reeled in girls with big dreams along the way. I liked imagining my mother in a long dress welcoming people into a big top under a billowing tent with a live circus band harrumphing behind her. I imagined her in the excitement of the drama, far away from the brothers who had taught her to smoke

Joy Harjo

cigarettes when she was nine years old so she wouldn't tell on them and get them in trouble. I see her laughing and feeling more like herself than she ever did in the shacks of borrowed homes she grew up in. I caught her dream of wanting to join the circus. Because I was older, and not the type to wear shiny outfits that showed skin, and heavy makeup, I decided to learn the saxophone so I could join the circus band.

I asked my mother's one living brother about this marriage.

"We had to find her and go get her," he told me. "And we found her dancing in a bar in Independence."

I wonder what would have happened had my mother been given a coming-of-age ceremony, or her mother or hers—a ritual in which they were welcomed and given spiritual and physical gifts to help them navigate their lives as young women who would grow to become matriarchs, to become beloved leaders in their families and their communities.

My mother still might have run away to join the carnival, but it would have been less likely. Those with strong family and community ties tend to run in the direction of home when there is trouble.

Ritual is how we make a community, how we open the door for respect for the source of life. Ritual nourishes our young men and women with the resources they need for spiritual growth for development.

Even a poem can be a ritual, as can a song, or a book.

◆　◆　◆　◆　◆

Someone has to make it out alive, sang a grandfather
to his grandson, his granddaughter,
as he blew his most powerful song into the hearts of the children.

There it would be hidden from the soldiers,
Who would take them miles, rivers, and mountains
                    from the navel cord place of the origin story.
He knew one day, far day, the grandchildren would return,
    generations later
over slick highways   constructed over old trails
Through walls of laws meant to hamper or destroy, over stones
bearing libraries of the winds.
He sang us back
            to our home place from which we were stolen
                        in these smoky green hills.

◆　◆　◆　◆　◆

"YOUR MOTHER SAID SHE KNEW you would make it," my sister-in-law told me. "She said that you knew how to survive. The others needed her more."

If I consider that my purpose with her in this life was to stand beside her as her witness, her advisor, then I find peace.
If I take away all the mothering expectations implied in the word "mother," then my mother becomes a human being. I make peace with my personal story of mothering.
I am honored to have served my mother.
I am honored to be a mother.

In our tribal nation's original teachings mothers, *ecke*, are blessed. Women are honored as co-creators of the future with men.

When we were colonized, female deities were deliberately disappeared from our indigenous stories. There is no female figure in

Christianity's Trinity. Mothers lost their place next to the fathers. They were treated as property. Those roles in society filled by women and mothers, positions like teachers and childcare workers, became the least respected and valued even though they are the most crucial.

The word "mother" wants to take over this whole story, and there is no combination of words, sentences, or paragraphs that could carry that weight, that story, and how it was borne from one mother to the next, from generations, from the beginning.

When I speak with a close friend, she tells me her mother is taking over her book of poetry, and the book isn't supposed to be about her, though she is part of the history. Is this the nature of mothers and mothering? Does each generation carry forth the wounding that needs to be healed, from mother to mother, cooking pot to cooking pot, song to poetry, and poetry to beadwork, until one day in eternity we will understand what we have created together?

◆　◆　◆　◆　◆

POET WARRIOR WRITES IN HER notebook in the tree:

Then as it was told, she had grown into a poet.
She became a word warrior, fighting a monster—
with knowledge that unfolded in words
that could be hidden
in plain sight.

No one else could see he was a monster.
Society commended him

for taking on a wife
who had been married,
and who had more children than could be counted.

Then, as it was told in the old stories,
Poet Warrior was given a poem
that gave her power to run faster than the monster.
The poem gave her the words to call out
for assistance.

And in the poem Poet Warrior
called to the winds, her relatives.
They flew into her lungs.
She called on the panther
who showed up in the poem,
sleek and black.
She climbed on panther's back.

That morning after her mother left for work,
the monster came into the room after her.
With the power of wind and panther
she escaped over bare flat lands
to the other side of tall, spiked mountains.
She made it
to the enclave of elder warriors
who used their practice of artmaking
to speak truth and fight for justice for Native people.
They took her in and taught her.

◆ ◆ ◆ ◆ ◆

Joy Harjo

WHEN WE ARE CHILDREN, OUR parents are gods. They preside over our kingdom, which might be located in a house, an apartment, or even a single room or a car, wherever it is they root together. They have control, even if they are out of control. There are many kingdoms on a suburban street, in a city, in an apartment building, or along a country road. When I travel through a city, a town, countryside, or someplace else here or in another part of the world and pass by rows and rows of abodes, I think about all those small kingdoms, each hidden behind a doorway, behind each lighted or dark window. I think of all the stories we make and are making, each grandparent, parent, and child, and how each is rooted to earth and time.

I will never forget coming up to a stoplight in Kolkata, India, and there on the traffic island in the middle of the street, a family had made a home of materials they had scavenged from the dump. During the momentary stop I had a brief window to a life, a family. Pans hung neatly on the wall. Mother's hair was pulled up and tied as she cooked the scant offering for dinner. Father held his baby daughter on his knee, and there she was, precious in her yellow dress wrapped in her father's loving arms. The light changed. Then we were gone.

I still think about this family, pray for them. I wonder how old the girl is now, if the family is okay, if they are still there on that traffic island. I wonder of what use is poetry and writing, and how my words can matter if they cannot help this family.

◆　◆　◆　◆　◆

AFTER MY STEPFATHER'S FUNERAL, I sat out in my mother's yard with my stepsister, his daughter, who was near the same age as my mother. She had been like a mother to me as I navigated the difficult years in his house. He was her monster even as he was her father, so she knew the story and had relived it with me. She survived her growing up with him, also by fleeing.

We sat together in her car while everyone else gathered and ate in the house. The mood in the trailer home was rather celebratory. She confided to me that her grandfather, my stepfather's father, used to drink heavily and shoot up the house every weekend. The neighbors would see my stepfather, when he was young, on the roof every Sunday morning, a little boy hitching up his pants, patching up bullet holes, not much older than my toddler sister whom he swung deftly by her leg to beat her. His mother spoiled him by doing everything for him, from cutting up his meat, even when he was a grown man, to giving him anything he asked for even if it caused her great sacrifice. We agreed that such wildly divergent parenting could give birth to such a man, as we tried to understand his life, how he had used his light.

My mother met him on a hunting trip with my father. He and my father worked together at the local airline. He was attracted to my mother's beauty, her vulnerability. My father's ability to attract women was legendary and envied in his male circle. While my father distracted himself with drink and other women, the soon-to-be stepfather moved in with romantic gestures and promises. My mother was lonesome, needy of romantic love. Their meeting churned in the disturbed waters of my parents' marriage. My parents soon divorced, and my mother ran away to Mexico to marry. In the wake the children whirled away in all directions though we went nowhere.

I did not ask for this stepfather. He was not my choice; it was my mother's decision to bring him into our lives. I do not want his story here with mine even now. Yet he is probably one of my greatest teachers. Because of him I learned to find myself in the

Joy Harjo

spiritual world. To escape him I grew an immense house of imagination. I decorated it. I planted a garden that would grow every year. I could find myself there living without fear. I even took flying lessons there. In that house I met and spoke with my ancestors who had gone on but who come back when we need their assistance. I found the ability to construct dreams with many kinds of materials. I saw the future; I saw the past. I battled monsters, then sat with them at the table to hear their stories. Everyone has a story. Even the monster has a story.

◆ ◆ ◆ ◆ ◆

FOR CALLING THE SPIRIT BACK FROM
WANDERING THE EARTH IN ITS HUMAN FEET

Put down that bag of potato chips, that white bread, that bottle
    of pop.
Turn off that cell phone, computer, and remote control.
Open the door, then close it behind you.
Take a breath offered by friendly winds. They travel the earth
    gathering essences of plants to clean.
Give back with gratitude.
If you sing it will give your spirit lift to fly to the stars' ears and
    back.
Acknowledge this earth who has cared for you since you were a
    dream planting itself precisely within your parents' desire.
Let your moccasin feet take you to the encampment of the
    guardians who have known you before time, who will be
    there after time.
They sit before the fire that has been there without time.
Let the earth stabilize your postcolonial insecure jitters.

Be respectful of the small insects, birds, and animal people
who accompany you. Ask their forgiveness for the harm we
humans have brought down upon them.

Don't worry.

The heart knows the way though there may be high-rises,
interstates, checkpoints, armed soldiers, massacres, wars,
and those who will despise you because they despise
themselves.

The journey might take you a few hours, a day, a year, a few
years, a hundred, a thousand or even more.

Watch your mind. Without training it might run away and leave
your heart for the immense human feast set by the thieves of
time.

Do not hold regrets.

When you find your way to the circle, to the fire kept burning by
the keepers of your soul, you will be welcomed.

You must clean yourself with cedar, sage, or other healing plant.

Cut the ties you have to failure and shame.

Let go the pain you are holding in your mind, your shoulders,
your heart, all the way to your feet. Let go the pain of your
ancestors to make way for those who are heading in our
direction.

Ask for forgiveness.

Call upon the help of those who love you.

Call yourself back. You might find yourself caught in corners
and creases of shame, judgment, and human abuse.

You must call in a way that your spirit will want to return. Speak
to it as you would to a beloved child.

Welcome your spirit back from its wandering. It will return in
pieces, in tatters. Gather them together. They will be so
happy to be found after being lost for so long.

Joy Harjo

Your spirit will need to sleep awhile after it is bathed and given
    clean clothes.
Now you can have a party. Invite everyone you know who loves
    you and supports you. Keep room for those who have no
    place else to go.
Make a giveaway, and remember, keep the speeches short.
Then, you must do this: help the next person find their way
    through the dark.

Part Three

A POSTCOLONIAL TALE

Sunrise, as you enter the houses of everyone here, find us.
We've been crashing for days, or has it been years.
Find us, beneath the shadow of this yearning mountain, crying
　　here.
We have been sick with sour longings, and the jangling of fears.
Our spirits rise up in the dark, because they hear
Doves in cottonwoods calling forth the sun.
We struggled with a monster and lost.
Our bodies were tossed in the pile of kill.
We were ashamed, and we told ourselves for a thousand years,
We didn't deserve anything but this—
And one day, in relentless eternity, our spirits discerned
　　movement of prayers
Carried toward the sun.
And this morning we are able to stand with all the rest
And welcome you here.
We move with the lightness of being, and we will go
Where there's a place for us.

◆　◆　◆　◆　◆

IN 1969 I EMBRACED AN opportunity to receive nursing assistant training at St. Vincent Hospital in Santa Fe. As one of the two top graduating students in that eight-week program, I had my choice of departments and chose pediatrics. Just a year earlier I had been cleaning rooms at St. John's Hospital in Tulsa, work I loved especially because my working partner, whom I'll call Ella Mae, was one of the best and most hardworking employees in the hospital. She trained me, unofficially and for no extra pay. We dusted, cleaned, and swept hospital rooms and hallways. She made the physically rough job joyful because she brought the best of herself to every task she undertook, even to the way she wielded a hot comb to straighten her daughter's hair. I can still smell the singe and the grease from the comb that was heated on the stove. I hear the laughter as stories unwound. She lived near where my parents briefly owned a bar, north of Apache. My father and his party friends destroyed that bar by running into it with my father's truck in the very early hours of the morning.

From the cleaners' point of view, we had our pulse on all the social levels of the hospital, from the laundry staff in the hot basement to the doctors walking on water through the hallways. Even though we were just cleaners, we visited with the patients, some of whom got to know us and looked forward to seeing us, especially Ella Mae. I was her quiet shadow, but I had muscle and will, and I knew how to work hard.

Later, as a nursing assistant at St. Vincent's, my job was to handle routine patient care, like bathing, taking vital signs, and assisting patients with eating, walking, and repositioning. Nursing assistants also provided and emptied bedpans as well as restocked supplies. We worked with every age from newborns who had been born outside the hospital, to teens. My favorite shift was from three P.M. to eleven P.M. I usually walked to work, about a mile through downtown Santa Fe. I would take my son to the Spanish family who took care of him, where he learned to speak Spanish before English. And then I walked the rest of the way up Palace Avenue, past the Plaza, which was always filled with older Spanish and Native men—who can be worse gossips than women—to the hospital. I paid gas money to a coworker who always drove me to pick up my son, then home.

Joy Harjo

This hospital work engaged me in a way nothing else had to that point. My innate impulse is healing, which is also standing up for justice, which can heal hearts and nations.

When I walked into each child's room, I felt a sacred tenderness. Children are fresher from our spiritual home. And when they are ill, highly vibrating spiritual helpers crowd the room to help. You can feel them. For children to suffer is nearly unbearable because no matter how you tell the story, it will never make sense. There is no explanation that will ameliorate the suffering of either the children or their parents. There is only kindness and being present in your prayerful being.

One night, after all the patients had been fed and had received their medications, and visiting hours were over, I sat by the bed of a little boy who was finally beginning to doze. I don't remember the extent of his illness or injuries. I sat there in the twilight, just being with him. The nurse who oversaw the unit came in. She was my favorite nurse there. Her name was Mildred Alderete. I can still feel her walking in with her low-heeled and cushioned white nurse shoes, her particular soft sway. She was always methodical in her observations and words. She looked over the boy and leafed quietly through his most recent sheet of records. Then she turned to me and said something that I cannot exactly recall. I hear the lift of her Caribbean patois as she spoke softly. It was something like this:

We are meeting here in a sacred place. Healing is a sacred art. I have been watching you and see that this work as a nursing assistant matters to you. Always take care of this gift I perceive in you—I see it in the way you look after the patients. I have no doubt you will do well in your profession. Remember us here and come back and see us.

I had been accepted as a pre-med student at the University of New Mexico and had given my notice to St. Vincent's. I loved my work in the hospital, in the care and healing of the patients. Her words kept me steadied many times, when I thought I might not make it through the night to the next morning.

I took up this work again when I began writing poetry, though I didn't always see it that way.

◆ ◆ ◆ ◆ ◆

OFTEN DURING THOSE DAYS AND nights I felt lost. I was far away from any close family, walking the road alone with no place to go except to return to the cheap housing I could barely afford in that Spanish and Indian town. I didn't feel much like an artist in those days, yet art is what sustained my spirit when I felt emptied and overwhelmed. When I had graduated high school from the Institute of American Indian Arts (IAIA), with Secretary of the Interior Stewart Udall as our commencement speaker, I hadn't returned directly to Oklahoma. My belly was swelling as I left campus with our drama and dance troupe to tour and perform in the Pacific Northwest for nearly a month. I kept the pregnancy hidden under loose shirts that covered my tight-fitting dance attire. I missed the collective family I had made at school after I returned to Oklahoma to give birth.

I had no sense of my future as I stepped one foot in front of the other through the slit of time between the late 1960s and very early '70s and found my way once again in the refuge of Santa Fe. I worked at whatever job I could get, from being an attendant at a gas station to teaching dance at a health club to working in the hospital. I'd go home, cook, clean, tend to my son or sometimes my son and stepdaughter. I reconnected with some of my old friends from IAIA who had either stayed in Santa Fe or moved back after we graduated.

Beadle wore all black, before this became fashionable, before goth, and was as thin as a stick. He was a brilliant painter from somewhere far north. There was Peter B. Jones (Seneca), who still makes pottery figures of those who people his reservation and his imagination. They carry wisdom, humor, and images that feed the spirit of his homelands. Larry Ahvakana already was inventive with his stunning original Inupiaq creations. I always remember how Gloria Bird (Spokane) and her husband, Harold Littlebird (Laguna and Santo Domingo Pueblo), would drive up to our gatherings on their bicycles, their daughters strapped to their backs. Harold is a potter and a poet who once when a group of us were flying to Phoenix for a conference walked up and down the airplane aisle with his pottery in his arms to offer pieces for sale to the passengers. We teased him about his Pueblo ways. Gloria wrote poetry. I quietly sketched and tried out for parts in the Santa Fe Little Theater. Years later Gloria and I edited a Norton anthology of Native North American women's writings, *Reinventing the Enemy's Language*.

In those early years as young artists, we'd often meet around a table in one of our homes, drawing together in our sketchpads, our children playing about us, and we'd talk about the state of Native art, our families, the emerging Native rights movement, and the love of our communities, their struggles. As we huddled over our art, our plates of food, our drinks, we'd tease and laugh, even as we'd discuss the times that were coming.

We all knew those who stayed close to home, who were keeping our cultural ways together despite the pressure to change. Many were our kin. They were the ones who used our languages, interacted with plants, and knew the seasonal essence of our living. They stayed close to the earth and kept the earth's altars. They humbly kept our teachings safe.

As we discussed among ourselves, we began to consider ourselves to be a kind of hybrid: not the confused, worn-out trope of Indians caught between two worlds, but committed artists rooted in our individual tribal nations who created within a dynamic process of cultural, conceptual interchange of provocative ideas, images, and movements. We agreed, for instance, that we could be inspired by Jimi Hendrix, by his artistry and his conceptual performances. We could borrow or be inspired, just like mainstream artists, who have always shared across time and culture. We could merge outsider sounds and ideas with our classical tribal expressions and make fresh musical art. We talked about how our painting teacher Fritz Scholder was influenced by the painter Francis Bacon, whose images emerged from the shadow parts of a post–World War Two imagination. Those disturbed symbolic images fitted our experiences. We could find our own symbols and interpret racialized postcolonial rage to creatively express the despair of generational grief and loss.

It was usually late at night as the children dropped to sleep on soft pallets made of blankets on the floor next to us or slept with their heads cradled on our laps, that we shared the stories of prophecies and warnings. We had heard that we were moving toward tremendous tests of famine, floods, and fires if we did not change our ways, if we forgot our original teachings and did not move forward respectfully and in relationship to the living world around us. There could become times when grandparents would throw their grandchildren away for greed. They would then become the same as the colonizers and would be the ones to take down and disparage our cultural traditions. Our Old Ones would then no longer recognize us. We would grow ears that could no longer hear them. We would be overcome with greed. The Earth would turn to her side to look away, as we lost balance, as female power was eroded.

Then someone would tell a joke to shift the weight, we'd put on music and snack on our potluck leftovers, and finally we'd go our separate ways into our lives. Yet we stayed connected even if we lost track of each other intermittently through the years. Our generation came in as a family; we will leave as a family. That story continues with successive generations. Our children and grandchildren now gather on the internet, as we did at the kitchen table, sharing their innovations on social media, making change as they hold up their part of the world.

◆　◆　◆　◆　◆

I ENTERED THE UNIVERSITY OF New Mexico as a pre-med major, intent on fulfilling my interest in healing. That fell away after my first semester with a schedule packed with science classes for which I had no preparation. By second semester I was back in the art studios. My first years at the university I painted through pain, through worrying about how I was going to buy the children new shoes. I painted during a revolution, and I painted when I had no words. I painted when I wasn't sure I could make it each step home from a panic that would overtake my breath and feed me with thoughts of suicide. I painted. I painted as I loved my children without question and because of what the painting was teaching me, to keep beauty moving in my hands, through my bloodstream, through my perceptions as I walked through the inner wars of historical trauma.

As I painted in the middle of the night, when it was quiet and all I could hear were my children's deep-sleep breathing and the voice of the cricket who lived in the corner of the room, the spiritual world greeted me in color, line, and meaning. There my spirit would emerge dressed in love. I was no longer judging myself unworthy. I saw that wide circle of ancestors who gave me inspiration and strength to continue. It was not about me. It was about us.

We are spoken to by the Old Ones through the arts, as we make art and as we appreciate the artistic creations of others. Every age of my life is connected by drawings, paintings, and art that inspired me. I decorated my daughter's crib with reproduction plates of paintings by Monet, Chagall, and Degas that I unglued from my art history textbooks. One of my favorite paintings is what is known as the "Chinese Horse" from the Lascaux caves in

One of my drawings from that time of Luther
Standing Bear, a Ponca civil rights leader

Joy Harjo

France. I hung that on my wall. I would later possess the paintings by my grandmother Naomi Harjo that hung in our home when my father still lived with us. I only have one of my drawings left from that time, a detailed pencil portrait of Luther Standing Bear (Ponca), who was at the forefront of progressive change, a civil rights leader who argued that Natives are human, worthy of human rights. I admired him.

My plan was to make a gallery of paintings and drawings of Native leaders to inspire. Many of them would be of leaders and warriors whose names are unfamiliar, like Chitto Harjo, who stood with Hickory Ground warriors for traditional values and governance against unlawful interference by the American government to force statehood and allotment. They would be of those Native women who would get up and make breakfast and lunches to send with their children, head off to work, or stay home, and humbly inspire their family and community. Some of them were artists in traditional arts like basketwork, regalia design, and beadwork; they were the ones who were the tremendously powerful heart of our nations.

◆　◆　◆　◆　◆

I DIDN'T PLAN ON BECOMING a poet. I was not easy with words. I was the girl with her hair in her eyes, her head down as she focused on making her way through the labyrinth of gender and race while she raised children, got an education, created, and worked. In a community of full-bloods, I was not a full-blood. I was an anomaly, because in those times in southwest Indian communities hardly anyone married or had children outside the Pueblo or the tight-knit Athabascan communities of Navajo or Apache. I was female and had no family in the community to circle around me. I was far from home. I knew who I was, however: a full Muscogee Creek citizen whose people knew her, and who loved her people.

I found community in the Kiva Club, which was the Native student club at the University of New Mexico, and with friends I acquired as I made art, began writing poetry, and attended feminist events on campus. Some of my closest friends were Navajo drag queens who taught me to accept the contradictions within myself and laugh hard about them and with them, as they bravely were themselves. The seed for my poetry writing was rooted in that circle of Old Ones in my tribal nation in Oklahoma, and it emerged and broke through to stand with young Indian artists in Santa Fe. I blossomed within that brave, brilliant, hilarious, and dedicated circle of friends and fellow students of the Kiva Club. It had been founded as a social club for American Indian students, and then our generation politicized it and the club became our headquarters for social change.

Poetry is a tool for navigating transformation, and we needed poets and poetry to make community and inner change. What led me toward the practice of poetry as a tool for justice was hearing the poetry of Simon Ortiz, an Acoma poet, as he read his original poetry on a local radio station. Until hearing him, I didn't know that we Natives could write poetry that was of our lives, our struggles, our revelations. Ortiz's poetry was personal, political, and historical, spoken in everyday language used in our tribal communities. I began writing, tentatively at first.

Ortiz introduced me to the poetry of Leslie Marmon Silko from Laguna Pueblo. I didn't know she was a novelist and short story writer. I knew her first as a poet. I met her when she was visiting home in New Mexico, all the way from Ketchikan, Alaska, where she had moved with her husband, John Silko. It was there

Joy Harjo

she was writing her breakthrough novel *Ceremony*, as the sky rained and rained and never let up. She was lonely for the dry air and colorful mesas of her southwest. We began a correspondence.

Learning the Navajo language for my "foreign" language requirement gave me a renewed sense of the power inherent in language and what language is capable of translating, as I wrote in the English language. Navajo language fed my early poetry. I did not know my own Mvskoke language because my father's mother passed before he learned to speak. Yet, many of those just a generation younger knew many indigenous languages, even as they might also have spoken English and Spanish and/or French.

I went to poetry readings sponsored by the English Department and heard many poets, including Galway Kinnell, who stunned me with his recitation of his poem "The Bear." He transformed into a bear as he read. I was fed by his exquisite and heartbreaking oratory, just as my ears were often compelled by the speeches given to the press by local Native elders standing up for justice, by eloquent testimonies I heard from community members attesting to the validity of the sacredness of land to corporations that were determined to take whatever they could in natural resources—and usually did. I remember the poet Ai and her powerful introverted poetry as it stood next to Anne Waldman's punchy oracular proclamations of poetry.

I was one of the Kiva Club women who cooked, printed flyers, cared for children, went to classes, studied, and marched. I remember my friend Mary's husband coming from Isleta Pueblo to pick her up from our club office on campus, with the family pet pig squealing and sliding back and forth in the bed of the pickup truck.

Our members organized in local tribal communities to take

back our governments, our schools, our essential rights. We were involved in tribal demonstration schools instituting curriculum, language, and tribal values. We marched in support of basic human rights for Native peoples. We sat in on negotiations by huge energy companies that fought for development of uranium, coal, oil, and other resources even if it meant mass destruction of Native lands.

We began to institute practices of sovereignty in all its many aspects, including language, tribal law and the courts, and education, and began investigating intellectual and cultural property rights. For some of us our art was the primary tool of activism. It was in this atmosphere of rising up that our arts flourished. It was there that I began writing poetry, for justice.

One of my earliest poems commemorated the short life of the young Navajo activist Alva Mae Benson, whom I admired as she worked quietly poised behind the scenes, often with a baby on her hip, organizing and supporting various events on behalf of the quality of life for community people.

FOR ALVA BENSON, AND FOR THOSE
WHO HAVE LEARNED TO SPEAK

And the ground spoke when she was born.
Her mother heard it. In Navajo she answered
as she squatted down against the earth
to give birth. It was now when it happened,
now giving birth to itself again and again
between the legs of women.

Or maybe it was the Indian Hospital
in Gallup. The ground still spoke beneath
mortar and concrete. She strained against the

metal stirrups, and they tied her hands down
because she still spoke with them when they
muffled her screams. But her body went on
talking and the child was born into their
hands, and the child learned to speak
both voices.

She grew up talking in Navajo, in English
and watched the earth around her shift and change
with the people in the towns and in the cities
learning not to hear the ground as it spun around
beneath them. She learned to speak for the ground,
the voice coming through her like roots that
have long hungered for water. Her own daughter
was born, as she had been, in either place
or all places, so she could leave, leap
into the sound she had always heard,
a voice like water, like the gods weaving
against sundown in a scarlet light.

The child now hears names in her sleep.
They change into other names, and into others.
It is the ground murmuring, and Mount St. Helens
erupts as the harmonic motion of a child turning
inside her mother's belly waiting to be born
to begin another time.

And we go on, keep giving birth and watch
ourselves die, over and over.
And the ground spinning beneath us
goes on talking.

♦ ♦ ♦ ♦ ♦

IT WAS IN THESE EARLY stages of writing poetry that I wondered about the ways in which poetry had appeared and functioned traditionally in my own tribal nation. I came to understand that we have a rich tradition of poetry, most of it in songwriting and oratory. I knew about the poetry of Alexander Posey. However, I questioned how poetry had appeared in these indigenous lands before colonization; and as a way to decolonize my approaches to poetry, I looked about for poems written in English by poets whose roots and cultures predated English-speaking colonizers. I found a chapbook called *Ride Me, Memory*, which was written by the poet Kofi Awoonor and published in 1973 by the Greenfield Review Press. Awoonor, who was born in 1935 and died in 2013, was Ghanaian, of the Ewe people. Indigenous orality was the foundation of his poems. And like the poets of his tradition, Awoonor engaged actively in the political landscape as a truth teller.

The poetry of Ugandan poet Okot p'Bitek influenced me profoundly; and meeting him in person in the late 1970s was a highlight of my early years of becoming a poet. His poem sequence *Song of Lawino* is one of the world's classic achievements in poetry. It was originally written in the Acholi dialect of southern Luo. His narrative poem is driven by the powerful voice of Lawino, a respected woman in her community. She eloquently upbraids her husband, Ocol, for his philandering and for his seduction by western ways that precipitate ruin in village life.

In Okot p'Bitek's poetry there was such an exact social correspondence with our tribal communities, how we had changed and were being changed by colonization to the extent that it was difficult to remember who we were or have control over who we were becoming as individuals or as tribal nations. Lawino tells the truth of the changes that were destroying village life, against her husband's weak protestations.

My husband says
I am useless
Because I waste time,
He quarrels
Because, he says,
I am never punctual.
He says, I have no time to waste.
He tells me
Time is money.

Ocol does not chat
With me,
He never jokes
With anybody,
He says
He has no time
To sit around the evening fire.

When my husband
Is reading a new book
Or when he is
Sitting in his sofa,
His face covered up
Completely with the big
  newspaper
So that he looks
Like a corpse,

Like a lone corpse
In the tomb,

He is so silent!
His mouth begins
To decay!

◆　◆　◆　◆　◆

SOME NIGHTS I DID NOT know what would happen if I took
my hand off the paintbrush, typewriter, or pen. I would look over
at my sweet babies sleeping. I did not want them to inherit this
struggle, this fight that was more than me, a fight that began back
when we were separated violently from the earth, our mother,
from her knowledge. If I were to give in to the terror there would
be no one there for them, or for me.

Creating was prayer.
I followed one word after another.
One image and then another.
Here on a tangled rectangle of a page stood a dreaming house.
Here I made a room in which I could speak and say whatever
came to me to speak. Here I could sing, and it would not be
forbidden to be:

breathing and singing girl, history, the myth of dying and
returning, a burning bird with a comet tail, a baby who could
not stop crying, a girl running away, too light, too dark, too
wrong, too right, taken for a ride on a moonlight night, a woman
with children on her back running, always running uptight,
outta sight, if you're brown get down, down, down—

I decided right then, during those long nights, that if my creative work did anything in this world, I wanted Indians to be seen
as human beings.

◆　◆　◆　◆　◆

Poet Warrior reached for a gun.
She was given a paintbrush,
A saxophone, a pen.
These will be your instruments of power
The Old Ones said.
Though the gun gleamed and pranced
As a tool of takeover by governments
Even as it danced
Through the imaginations of revolutionaries
As the perfect tool for social change.
Do not be fooled, they told her.
Violence might be louder, tougher
And is often good looking.
The power of insight and compassion
Is fiercely humble and helpful.
Be ready for what the story of your age demands:
You will be tested.
There will be jealousy, envy,
But the most difficult enemies will be
From your closest circle
Even your family.
You must act in a manner
That will cause no harm
To anyone, seven generations back
Or forward.

* * * * *

MANY NIGHTS I FELT DARK presences as they pulled on me to take me with them. I'd struggle. One night I screamed aloud in the middle of the demon fight, when I was camped out with friends after attending a Native sovereignty conference and we were sleeping. They knew what to do for such hauntings and took me the next morning to a medicine man in the Four Corners area. The demons scattered and I did not see them again until one night, months later. They grabbed me and began their drag of me through astral mud to steal me. I fought them.

Then I heard the voice of the knowing. "Raise your vibration. Make it faster."

They helped sing a humming sound through me. With that protection song the demons fell away. That was the last time I saw them with their grasping sharp claws.

* * * * *

WE KEEP OUR VIBRATION HIGHER by prayer, by kindness, by taking care of what we were given to do, by cleaning ourselves of negative thoughts that originate within or come from others, by cleaning with water, by humility, by being in the real world, away from concrete and square buildings, by speaking only that which holds truth.

* * * * *

ONCE I ASSISTED MY *KUMU*, or teacher, in a *ho'oponopono* healing. I stood next to her in the center of the circle of partic- ipants, each gathered to forgive someone or something in their

Joy Harjo

lives, to let go. With *pule*, or prayer, she raised up the energy for healing. My energy rose up to match hers. I then saw as she saw. Behind each person stood another person or persons who had come forth to be forgiven, emerged from time or from the other side, each attached to a participant in the circle. Some were relatives, others who had transgressed were strangers. There had been violent incidents, words. Some went back years, others were fresh. Many of those in line or circling the participants were in tears. I saw with such detail. Then, as quickly as it appeared, the vision was gone.

◆　◆　◆　◆　◆

There you are, voice, said Poet Warrior as she began
Writing poetry because there was no other way to speak.
It was unlike any voice from within her.
It wasn't her little girl voice, or the defensive
Teenage girl voice.
Or the tamped down so I don't get hurt voice.
Or the leave me alone voice.
She didn't know this voice at first.
She watched it emerge from afar.
Admiring it and at once fearful of it.
It was a red bird on a branch of wind.
It was a whirling rainbow
In the hand of a child.
It was a trail of ancestors, walking and on horseback
Approaching and crossing
A raincloud in ever changing light.
Where did you come from, she asked the voice?
If you follow me, said the voice, without words

You will know where I came from, who I am
And where I am going in a time made of willow branches.
And the voice kept going, and Poet Warrior kept following no
    matter
Her restless life in the chaos of the story field.

◆ ◆ ◆ ◆ ◆

I APPEARED TO HAVE IT together. I took care of my babies, I went to classes full time with perfect attendance and began making straight A's, while at the same time I worked a job and earned solid evaluations. But I was not free of history, and sometimes I told myself I just needed a break.

Most of us Indian students liked to hang out with each other, let loose, play pool or dance a little. Some of us drank. Drinking felt good at first, loosened the hold of the tension of walking the daily race obstacles, for some of us: the race line. Those of us who never talked became sociable, funny, as the shyness slipped from our shoulders. This was the part that hooked us: the illusion of the freedom of being. Just when we were having fun, in that warm haze of belonging, then came the hard part. The fights began. Someone's husband planted a kiss on someone's girlfriend. Old tribal enmities took hold. I'd get challenged to a fight because I was light. I knew how to run and could disappear into a crowd. Some would pass out and we'd paint them up. Others crawled home. Or worse, they wouldn't make it home at all. We were the lost children of the boarding school generation, the children of those stolen as babies from their parents' and grandparents' arms.

Somehow, we made it through those years. I was in a car once that was being driven up the wrong side of the interstate at three in the morning. I ran the streets in the dark after the bar closed to

Joy Harjo

get away from violence while running into it. I saw guns, knives drawn, and blood. Still, we had fun, made lifelong friends, and when we visit now, we call it a good run at living.

◆　◆　◆　◆　◆

THERE'S NO WAY TO DESCRIBE that interconnected rhythm that moves through a crowd of Native friends who are happy to see each other, as they share stories, laugh and laugh some more, so much that they are bent over with impossible laughter and a happiness that can only come from suffering and surviving the postcolonial world together.

That rhythm is shaped like a wave, signaled by familiar phrases that make no sense to anyone else but us.

"Ayyyeeee." "Ohhhhhh." "Like that . . ." "Heyla . . ."
"That's what she said."

◆　◆　◆　◆　◆

ONE NIGHT AFTER A LONG day of sessions at an Indian education conference in Oklahoma City, after visiting and partying a little in the hotel bar, a carload of us decided to head out to a forty-niner near Carnegie. These singing and socializing parties took place after bars closed. They were usually held far from the city, far from where anyone could interrupt or arrest us for the crime of being Indian. Police always followed us wherever we gathered. They lined up outside Indian bars near closing to pick us off.

There were always complicated sets of instructions to get to these forty-nine sites. In Albuquerque we used to go up into the

Juan Tabo picnic area of the Sandia Mountains until the police began following us there; then we moved to the West Mesa, which is now filled with subdivision homes. Often we would drive many dirt roads deeper and deeper into the woods or prairie for freedom.

On the way that night to Carnegie, we listened to the driver's eight-track player jamming powwow music. His uncle was the most in-demand powwow emcee. They're picked for their joking abilities, their knowledge of powwow, and their standing in their communities.

All tribal.
Everyone out there. Grandma too.
Grab grandpa before that woman eyeing him across the floor
    decides to take him for a spin.
Suck in your gut in a good way.
Listen up.
Everybody, dance.

We were nearing the turnoff to Carnegie when we saw the red lights and heard the sirens of the highway patrol. We'd been doing the speed limit. We knew we were being stopped because we were Indian.

The policemen demanded the driver's license and stared with their flashlights into our faces. Then they scanned the floorboards, looking for six-packs, cases, and empties. We were prepared. There were none. Then they made all of us get out of the car.

We stood next to the interstate while they opened the trunk and searched. We knew they could do anything to us they wanted. If we protested, they would take us in on made-up charges, after roughing us up first and charging us with resisting arrest. We'd been through this before. We kept our eyes down to save ourselves

Joy Harjo

in the flashlight glare as we felt the whizz of Saturday night traffic passing by, smelled the tallgrass prairies glistening with humidity. The anxiety froze us in place.

We knew all the reasons that compelled the officers to turn on the lights and motion us over on the highway. One Indian was all Indians. To them, we were all lawbreakers. They looked for any excuse to let loose on us: a smart mouth, belligerence, or a single muscle flickering with anger or fear, to give them reason to beat on us. At the root of the hatred was the unconscious knowledge that their ancestors had killed and stolen land and resources that didn't belong to them. If we grew in numbers, strength, or knowledge, we might turn and do to them what they had done—continued to do—to us.

They shut the trunk lid. There were two of them and a carload of us. They knew how to add. They let us go with a warning.

We drove the rest of the way with the windows open to clear our minds. How sweet to hear the singing emerge from the distance to greet us, to feel the winds moving cool relief across the grass.

We came out here just to be us, our laughter, our wounding, our happiness, our fighting, our primitive selves, our boarding school selves, our blanket-ass Indian selves, our stomp-dance shell-shaker selves. We came out here so we could be and so what if we party a little too much, if we love a little too thick, if we sing a little too loud, if we use our history books to build the fire, so what if we come out here to be renewed by stars, fire, and friends, so what—

◆　◆　◆　◆　◆

"SO WHAT," MILES DAVIS SANG on his horn in the blood fields, and sometimes the Indian jazzers elbowed a tune in between the powwow numbers.

THESE WESTERN PLAINS TRIBES KNEW how to do it. They were sophisticated. That forty-nine even had its own emcee. We drank Everclear and purple Kool-Aid mixed up in plastic-lined trash cans. We were far away from the highway patrol and happy not to be locked up just for being Indian.

Through the night we heard the classics:

"When the dance is over sweetheart, I will take you
home in my one-eyed Ford."

"Oh my dearest sweet loved one
How I miss you my dear
If you were only here
But you're so far away
If you were only here
I'd be OK"

"Oh my Blackjack Daisy
She got mad at me because I said hello to my old timer
But that's just OK with me"

"To hell with your old man
Come up and see me sometimes"

At four A.M. the emcee announced a men's shawl dance. This was something I'd never seen, men dancing a women's dance. The hosts had built a runway stage of crates and whatever wood scraps they could find. The girls lent their shawls. The young men lined up in a row and danced, each attempting to outdo the other as the drummers sang, yelled, and pounded on their cars. The dancers staggered and swirled. We laughed and laughed at such good fun. We had to admit that some of those men shawl dancers were almost as good as the women. And in that mix a few brave ones were men who chose to be women.

Somehow, everyone made it home, somehow.

◆　◆　◆　◆　◆

There she was, starting down the drinking road.
Poet Warrior had many companions as they swayed
To an unseen music.
She hid in the bushes to take a swig.
She even led a forty-nine dance once, she was told
But she didn't remember.
It felt good to let go.
The gut monster liked to drink and drink.
But he was becoming heavy
And one morning in that crack
Between heartbreak and dawn
She saw the road home clear,
Put down her bottle and took it.

◆　◆　◆　◆　◆

I RETURNED TO TEACH AT the Institute of American Indian Arts after graduating from the Iowa Writers' Workshop at the University of Iowa. I taught several creative writing classes, from poetry to fiction. One afternoon in the spring of 1980, I squeezed as many creative writing students as I could into my small Japanese-made truck with a camper. We headed to Albuquerque to spend the afternoon with Richard Hugo, a major American poet who had come to give a workshop and reading at the University of New Mexico. I'd been told of Hugo's luminosity, his compassion, his wry humor. I learned how generous he was as he met with my students and answered their questions about writing, poetry, and life in general. He treated them as equals in the creative field. That night we listened with hundreds as he spilled stories and read poetry to a packed auditorium.

I can still see my students lined up in the back row of the auditorium, listening to Hugo's poems and the poignant, witty stories that accompanied them. Hugo was a greeter at the door of poetry. He welcomed my students in as he did so many others. I was told that his funeral service in 1982 was packed with people he had met as he traveled about the country speaking and reading poetry. They were from the ordinary encounters of any traveler, people he met while checking into a hotel, the cleaners, servers, and attendants, and other travelers along the way. They shared that he had changed their lives.

As we gathered up to return to Santa Fe one of the students questioned, "Where's Nez?"

"She's at Okie's," someone answered. Okie's was the local biker, Indian, poet, and university student bar, located at the edge of campus.

So, we drove to Okie's first, to retrieve Nez, a brilliant young Navajo woman majoring in pottery. We were always concerned about her. She would disappear into her private suffering then reappear as if nothing had happened, but we would see the wear on her. Would she make it? And what does "make it" mean in the whole scheme of the world? Perhaps "not making it" in one world was making it in another.

When her spirit broke free as it did in her art making, she was raw and beautiful.

That night we became a Richard Hugo poem: a truck of Indian students headed to Okie Joe's bar to retrieve Nez from the clutches of companions of forgetfulness.

We all waited in the truck while I sent a student in to Okie's to find Nez. He didn't return. Next another volunteer, then another, until I was the only one left, and had to go into that place to bring everyone home.

Nez would not come with us. There she was a few days later, hard at work in the pottery studio, nodding a hello.

Another time I borrowed a school van and took my students to the Albuquerque Indian School to teach poetry to high school students. In teaching others, they were required to master the tools given to them in their classes, enough to share. My creative writing and literature classes at IAIA taught me about teaching.

When I taught at IAIA I moved freely and imaginatively as I constructed my lesson plans and led my classes. I did not get stalled in second-guessing my pedagogical choices and strategies as I would when I began teaching in the university system. Because the students were all Indians, we shared base assumptions about the world in which we were living. That generation of Indian students naturally valued the power of the word because they were raised up in or were only one generation separated from highly literate cultures that depended on well-constructed orality for law. Living storytelling still predominantly imparted values and culture.

Later on, when I began teaching in the university system, I lost myself. I attempted to remake myself to fit in a system in which I would never quite fit. I did not feel secure enough in myself to take an indigenous teaching strategy and refit it for my classroom. I was often the only Indian in my department or one of a few in a whole university staff. Indigenous peoples and our contributions were not present in the curriculum or literature.

I did my best but not without a deep inner struggle about the process. This issue came to a crisis when I was teaching at UCLA in the early part of 2000. I overheard a student complain to her visiting friend, who had come to my class to meet me because of my reputation as a poet, that she wished I taught the way I wrote poetry. I recalled how I had taught at IAIA and began to attempt to regain my center.

One way I met this challenge was to include orality and how it is present and at the root of every contemporary form of literature. In the last American literature course I taught at UCLA, "Decolonizing the American Mind," a class on contemporary American poets, I required the students to memorize one hundred lines of poetry by an American poet we had been studying, and then recite in class for their midterm. A short paper was also required on their choice of a poet and a poem. This news set the class into a flurry of protest at having to memorize so many lines. The advisor for the department told me she fielded a few requests by students to change the class so they would not have to memorize. I then met individually with each student. No one dropped. For two whole class periods during midterms students stood up one by one and recited poetry. What elation and surprise erupted from the class at the end of that two days because they experienced how the magic of poetry had lived and moved through them as they performed and listened. When the course was completed, they carried poetry within. I still hear from those students.

◆ ◆ ◆ ◆ ◆

I DID NOT WANT TO leave teaching at IAIA. The Albuquerque Indian School was under the control of the All Indian Pueblo Council, unlike IAIA, which was under the direction of the Bureau of Indian Affairs. The IAIA campus had originated as the Santa Fe Indian School, but in 1962 it was commandeered for an arts school for high school and post-graduate Indian students from all over the country. This change gave rise to long-lasting enmity and AIPC wanted the school back. They decided to close and tear down the Albuquerque Indian School and take back the Santa Fe campus.

Soon their staff from Albuquerque were in our offices, taking measurements, talking about new furnishings, as if we were not present at our desks or in our classrooms. I began suffering migraines and was getting an ulcer, problems I'd never encountered until the announcement. Those original school grounds were sacred to me and many others. I decided I had to resign for my health, before the IAIA campus was moved to temporary buildings behind a Catholic college in Santa Fe.

With the job loss, I became unmoored. I started a relationship that should never have even been a first date. Our lives did not fit in any direction, except for the need to escape, and escape we did in a U-Haul truck that nearly didn't make it up the infamous steep climb near Camp Verde, Arizona, heading for Tempe. This began a series of restless, but purposeful, moves I made over the course of thirty years that would take me as far away as Hawai'i before I would return to Oklahoma.

◆ ◆ ◆ ◆ ◆

A POSTCOLONIAL TALE

Every day is a reenactment of the creation story. We emerge from
dense unspeakable material, through the shimmering power of
dreaming stuff.

This is the first world, and the last.

Once we abandoned ourselves for television, the box that separates
the dreamer from the dreaming. It was as if we were stolen, put into
a bag carried on the back of a man who pretends to own the
earth and the sky. In the sack were all the people of the world. We
fought until there was a hole in the bag.

When we fell we were not aware of falling. We were driving to
work, or to the mall. The children were in school learning
subtraction with guns.

We found ourselves somewhere near the diminishing point
of civilization, not far from the trickster's bag of tricks. Everything
was as we imagined it. The earth and stars, every creature
and leaf imagined with us.

When we fell, we were not aware of falling. We were driving to
work or to the mall. The children were in school learning
subtraction with guns.

The imagining needs praise as does any living thing.
We are evidence of this praise.
And when we laugh, we're indestructible.
No story or song will translate

Joy Harjo

the full impact of falling,
or the inverse power of rising up.
Of rising up.

Our children put down their guns when we did to imagine with
    us.
We imagined the shining link between the heart and the sun.
We imagined tables of food for everyone.
We imagined the songs.

The imagination conversely illumines us, speaks with us, sings
with us, drums with us, loves us.

Part Four

DIAMOND LIGHT

* * * * *

AS I STARTED A NEW life in Arizona, I knew I was losing myself. Even a lost place within yourself is a place, albeit liminal, a kind of border town. You can make a temporary home if you need to from found materials and shreds of forgotten dreams, and you can even dress to appear somewhat ordinary as you run away, a refugee from yourself. I rolled up the map of my known world and set it aside for some kind of strange autonomy.

I was raising two young children and kept a structure that would support their needs. We were now in the desert making a home, even farther away from homelands and family. At that point in my life, my later twenties, Oklahoma meant a trek to heartbreak, to what began as a kind of refugee camp for Natives moved at gunpoint from the East, followed by droves of settlers who established their laws, their churches, and deemed us second-class citizens.

I kept close with my father, who was living in a beach town south of Houston near his Potawatomi girlfriend. He loved his grandchildren. I was able to string together a series of residencies in poets-in-the-schools programs, writing jobs, and an occasional poetry reading.

I was making a life as a poet though I was never sure what that would look like, as I was not the usual poet. I did not fit the image of poet or even Native, nor was I acting as a proper woman. I could have honored my difference; instead I got in my own way. I quit a part-time lecturer position, in the middle of the semester, because I was demoralized by the department chair calling me in for a one-on-one meeting in which he called me a "primitive poet" after opening my book and pointing out the rough simplicity of my poetry. I felt the meeting and his questions were meant to demean me. My sudden departure was without responsibility for the students or the others in the department. I did not take into account the overview and how my actions caused hardship.

I focused on the incredible desert of cacti and other growing things where my children and I were now living. These desert plants knew how to survive with very little rain. The way the winds navigated through sandy plains and over stones renewed my spirit. Mountains rose up in the distance and made a zigzag sky.

My children were slick otters of joy in these rough waters of living, though I worried constantly about having enough time for them, and about how I was going to meet all the expenses of living. I took my children nearly everywhere with me, to board meetings, poetry readings, and concerts. We always packed Hot Wheels cars, drawing materials, and snacks.

Writing was my portal to grace, an opening in which I could hear my ancestors speaking, in which I knew we were cared for no matter my inadequacies or failings. "Eagle Poem" was given to me after I emerged from a sweat lodge on a nearby reservation. When I say "given," I mean that after the four eagles circled over the lodge when we emerged, attracted by prayer and singing, the poem came to me in a kind of spiral circling, like an eagle in a wind drift. The poem would go on to bring eagle grace to those who read or listened. It was beyond me, something given that helped guide me to my path, when my path still appeared as a misty unknown road. It would be passed to my children, and their children.

I was elected to the board of the Phoenix Indian Center, and that community became my home. Harry Long, a beloved Muscogee Creek board member, impressed me with his kindness. He was a respected Methodist minister and, like many of our Mus-

Joy Harjo

cogee Creek people, was very cultural in his expression of faith. He showed a love for all of creation. I stood taller and was more myself around him. Another board member, Phyllis Bigpond, a tall Yuchi-Creek woman, reminded me of how much I missed home. She and Harry Long had the same qualities of the Old Ones, a warm-hearted wisdom and sense of connection, what we call *vnokeckv*.

I met up with many local Indians, including Josiah Moore (Tohono O'odham), an educator. The first time we met at a community event sponsored by the Indian Center, we waved to each other from a distance, walked up and greeted each other familiarly, then realized we hadn't met yet. We just picked up our conversation from where we had left off, in a somewhere ago. There are old connections like those whose origins we don't know.

We soon began traveling to cultural events around Phoenix and the reservations. The drive from Phoenix south to his home on the Gila River Reservation was a road of stories. Once he pointed to an area to the east of the highway. Years back a family from Oklahoma escaping the dust bowl had broken down there. His family had taken them in, fixed their wagon, and sent them on their way with food and a little money. My love of *waila*, or chicken-scratch music—a music made of a convergence of southern Arizona native music, German polkas, and mariachi bravado—came from attending dances held in the backyards of tribal members. The gossips put Josiah and me together, but we were just friends who similarly loved our communities and the stories that were always emerging as we worked in our respective fields for Native rights and for recognition of indigenous contributions to education and the arts.

◆　◆　◆　◆　◆

MY FAVORITE STORY WAS OF Josiah's uncle Russell Moore (1912–83), a gifted trombonist who used to play with the major big bands that crossed the country from east to west. Russell Moore played in Louis Armstrong's All-Stars band, as well as with Lionel Hampton, Sidney Bechet, and Papa Celestin, not to mention starting his own bands. His musician friends called him "Big Chief."

Josiah told me how his uncle would stop and play for the people at the reservation.

When he arrived home, he made sure a good meal was served for the band with all his favorites, including popovers, red chili, and *wakial cecemait* or cowboy tortillas. He loved seeing his family, feeling those hugs from his mother and aunts, who laughed as they teased him, and joining the smoking circle with his uncles. He enjoyed introducing the jazz band and his family to each other.

Those reservation concerts are my favorite places to visit in my imagination. There I pull up a chair, sit back under the stars, and listen. "Big Chief" Russell Moore could really let loose. And when he was there performing proudly for his community he was especially inspired. I wonder if he knew that southeastern Indian people contributed to the origin story of the music he loved so much, a music that gave him a life in which to create, dream, and do what he loved most. I hadn't picked up a saxophone yet in the early 1980s. It was on my list of things to do: Learn saxophone or take flight lessons. Both I equated with flying.

Years later, after Josiah had passed this world, his son, Jacob, arranged for me and other Native musicians to give a concert honoring the memory of "Big Chief" on the reservation. I was humbled to return to that desert of memory, to pay tribute to our ancestor musicians who had broken through the walls of racism, prejudice, and historical reckoning to make an original American music that still inspires us many, many years later.

I was once told by a researcher after a performance that there are more Native jazz players per population than any other ethnicity. The Native All-Stars Jazz Band would also have to include the Mvskoke/Kaw saxophone player, Jim Pepper. To talk about James G. Pepper, we have to go back, go way back, back to the heartlands of the Mvskoke people, backward along the backbone of the Trail of Tears from Alabama, Georgia, the whole of the South, to New Orleans—to Congo Square, the mythical navel cord place of the birth of jazz. You will find it by the sound of the turtle shell rattles tied around the legs of our women (though back then the rattles were of deer dew claws), as they stomp the swing of the call-and-response of the male singers, by the families and friends calling out to each other, enjoying the company, the dance, because Congo Square was the village of the Houma, a Muscogean tribal nation.

The story goes that this village became a meeting place, a dance place for many southeastern tribal groups who periodically traveled through the area. It was a meeting place as well for African tribal people who traveled their own trails of tears across the Atlantic, and for various European peoples who were attracted to the music, the meaning in the beat, the flight in song, and always the food wrapped in cloth and gourds, and the romantic potential walking about in those gatherings. This world of origins and peoples lived in the fat sound of Jim Pepper's wild and brilliant tenor saxophone.

It was not surprising that Jim Pepper picked up a horn and played what he found there in his lifelong study of saxophone, a study that took him from Oregon to Oklahoma to Alaska to New York to Europe and to Africa. He made a music of synthesis, like the synthesis that created blues and jazz. He included the Native American Church peyote chants that his grandfather Ralph Gilbert taught him in his music, side by side with the stomp dance of his mother's people. His jazz ancestry included John Coltrane, Ben Webster, Plains powwow, and other American dance forms.

Within a few years after landing in Tempe, Arizona, I would live briefly in Denver. There I picked up a tenor sax that someone had left behind for safekeeping in my apartment. I started with the G-Blues scale. Then I bought a King Super relatively cheap, and went from there, practicing daily, up and down scales, through exercises, then ventured into jazz standards. On a trip to perform poetry in New York City I decided to look up Jim. I went through three taxicab drivers before I found one who would drive me to his address in a dangerous neighborhood in Brooklyn. I took my soprano saxophone for a lesson, and we began our friendship.

"It's all about these old cats. No one sounds like them anymore," he said, something like that—And we listened to Ben Webster and Coleman Hawkins that first afternoon. I thought about how sounds are born of a time and history, how we come together, the sources of our beliefs, and even how we speak as we break bread together.

There would be other lessons after that when I'd visit the city. He treated me like a sister.

I put on Pepper's music when I need to be reminded where I came from in the saxophone story. His sound continues to feed my spirit. It is a fat sound, full of mischief, earthiness, stomp ground soul, all the ingredients that go into making a Mvskoke roots music.

Jim Pepper passed from this world on February 10, 1992.

Everywhere I go in the trail of Jim Pepper, he is remembered. He is remembered in Anchorage, Alaska, where he played his way through bars on those long, cold, rowdy Alaska winter nights. He is remembered in the Village Vanguard, where I last saw him as I listened at a small table with the poet Jayne Cortez. Jim was out of his mind, his horn screaming what his heart couldn't speak. His music continues to be remastered and played around the world.

Water spirit feeling
springin' round my head,
makes me feel glad
that I'm not dead.

When I pick up my horn and blow, I stand near him, an echo, a new song, in this postcolonial world.

I wouldn't be a horn player without Jim Pepper, this ancestor horn player.

◆　◆　◆　◆　◆

STOMP ALL NIGHT

Let's hear it for the sisters; they know how to stomp.
Up all night. Cook all day.
Give it to the brothers; they know how to sing.
In the circle all day. Up all night.

Round dance, chicken scratch, forty-nine, and stomp!
Bury my heart at Horseshoe Bend.
We pay for light, pay for water, next thing you know
We'll pay to breathe harder.

Let's hear it for the sisters; they know how to stomp.

Text all day. Talk all night.
Give it to the brothers; they know how to sing.
Love all night. Pay all day.

Vkvsamet hesaketmese pomvte
Mowe towekvs pokvhoyen yiceyvte
Mon vkerrickv heren
Pohkerricen vpeyeyvres

Let's hear it for the sisters; they know how to stomp.
Dance all night. Kids all day.
Give it to the brothers; they know how to sing.
Work all day. Kids all night.

Those grounds north of 40, keep their cool.
They're warm and friendly, and like to play pool.
The grounds south of 40, sing loose and sweet.
They're sure good looking, like pork meat.

Let's hear it for the sisters; they know how to stomp.
Up all night. Cook all day.
Give it to the brothers; they know how to sing.
Work all day. Up all night.

Stomp all night until the morning light.
The Trail of Tears ends here in the Muscogee Creek Nation
    Reservation.
Stomp all night until the morning light.
We take care of the songs; the songs will take care of us.

◆　◆　◆　◆　◆

Joy Harjo

Poet Warrior kept track of the traditional calendar
Even when she roamed far from her story of origin—
And there were times she was so far away
Even beyond the reach of words—
Of any words in Mvskoke or English—
She worried she would never find her way
Through the multiplication of square rooms, streets,
And backed up mind terrors—
But early every summer, just after the new moon
There in the fields of new corn
Of her imagination
Could be found the new year, the time of green corn
Where the people come together to celebrate
To begin anew—
"Leave behind you
everything that needs to be let go"
And we begin again, on good terms
With each other—
We let go what needs to be let go
And start our fires with ashes from the ceremony
With our good thoughts, our lifting up thoughts
Carried in song, dance, and prayer—
We say, see you soon in the tomorrow
Where we will meet again—
Though Poet Warrior was far away from the familiar shape of
    seasons
Green Corn gave her a sense of direction
The new year pointed her toward home—

❖   ❖   ❖   ❖   ❖

I COME UPON MYSELF AS a young woman sitting alone in the backyard of a suburban home in a middle-class neighborhood of a large southwestern city. Most of the homes in that subdivision had a pool out back, a necessity for the heat that frequently shot up into the triple digits. Desert nights are cool. Everyone becomes nocturnal. The children are in bed because they have school the next day.

I note that she wears a light jacket. It used to be nights she would write when the children were younger, now it's mornings, after they leave for school. She likes to be alone with the sounds of night. It's a suburb, so what she hears are a few dogs barking, traffic, neighbors talking, and a cricket who lives along the edge of the house and likes to sing.

As she listens into the dark, past the sounds of families, she realizes how far away she has come from herself. Though her spirit is happy in the desert, she and her little family are quite alone. They are making a life, though there are no roots here that tell her they belong. She takes care of the tasks of a daily routine of a house and a family and makes it work. She gets the children off to school, then sets up and writes poetry on her typewriter. She sends poems out and is working on a book of poetry. She works out with weights at the fitness center. The routine grounds her. She has friends. Yet there is an ache that scrapes at the bottom of her spirit. She is listening to it as I watch her.

One of her favorite things is to check the children out for a day from school and take them on an unexpected adventure, even just to the park and for ice cream. They are barely making it financially but when there's a little extra, that's how she likes to spend it.

She ponders how her daughter's father doesn't set out to destroy himself and everything around him with his drinking.

Like her and everyone else who partied, he just wants to hang for a while, share stories and laugh together. Then go home at a decent hour and wake up in the morning to the clean sound of doves and make a life of meaning. But something else takes hold. He is on a binge and at least he cannot find her here.

She admires the bougainvillea draped over from the neighbor's side of the wall. She thinks of a García Lorca poem she has been reading. His poems feel spiked like the desert plants, so aware of the rain because of the heat. When she hears the doves here murmuring close to sunrise, she thinks of his poem "Of the Dark Doves." The date palm next to her will have to stand in for the laurel tree.

> In the branches of the laurel tree
> I saw two dark doves
> One was the sun
> and one the moon
> Little neighbors I said
> where is my grave —
> In my tail said the sun
> On my throat said the moon
> And I who was walking
> with the land around my waist
> saw two snow eagles
> and a naked girl
> One was the other
> and the girl was none
> Little eagles I said
> where is my grave —
> In my tail said the sun
> On my throat said the moon

In the branches of the laurel tree
I saw two naked doves
One was the other
and both were none

by Federico García Lorca
Translated from the Spanish by Sarah Arvio

I am standing outside here to tell this part of the story because I do not know how to tell you about the Council, and how they approached me as that young woman, who sat reflecting on her life by the pool of water in the desert. The Council only appears when you are at a crossroads, when you are in danger of going far astray of your plan for your life, or something important or unseen has come up and they need your attention. They are not physical, though they have been known to knock on the door and when you go to answer, no one is there. Or they find you in your dreams.

I am nearly equally balanced between intuition and intellect. My mind is always grandstanding for attention and there are so many details of living that keep me in the mind-field. When that happens, the Old Ones come to me in my dreams to speak to me. I listen to my dreams, as did my grandmother.

The Council is essentially made up of Old Ones, in overseer positions. That's my take on it, and what do I know, other than what I perceive. Perception is always growing if you feed it, like a plant.

I saw them, but not with physical seeing, and I knew they were there, and I could hear them. It's not the same as "hearing voices." It's like dreaming awake. If you are a creative artist, you know what I mean. We create in the realm in which the Council appears. Fiction writers interact with their characters. Poets ride

Joy Harjo

time. Painters open perceptual doors with line or color. Musicians hear what can't be heard.

I felt their serious approach, and then there they were, seated in front of me in a semi-circle. A meeting by the Council means that this is a time of import. Pay attention. Something powerful is at work to bring them to you.

The Council imparted to me that it was time. It was time to turn in the direction of developing my spiritual gifts. (A spiritual gift could be involved in writing poetry, music, teaching, even fixing motors to the best of your ability.) I had wandered to the desert for a reason. I was always being taught in the physical, mental, and spiritual levels, but it was time to challenge me to a more rigorous standard.

Now I am sharing this with you because I want to take a look at this moment in my life to understand, so you might better understand yourself.

I was respectful. We nearly always have a choice. Every gift comes with responsibility. We can say yes or no.

I had sat with the question I knew they were going to ask me as they approached. I felt the cumulative heaviness of raising two children without support, the burden of a gift of writing that I didn't understand, except that I had to follow it when it made no sense to anyone. My family didn't understand my gift or me. I didn't fully comprehend it either. All I knew was that I had to go wherever it took me. Every place it took me I found something I needed, sort of an extended lifelong scavenger hunt game. I picked up a piece I needed in every location and I assumed that one day they would all fit together, and I would finally understand what it all means.

I sat respectfully as I listened to the Council. Then, with a deep breath, I told the Council no, I am not ready. I want to have fun.

I pull up closer, next to the nearly thirty-year-old self who just declined the opportunity offered by the circle of wise ones to develop. I want to understand her because this is a story of which I am most ashamed. I see her as she sits there in her jeans and scissored sweatshirt. I note here that yes, she is wearing jeans and a sweatshirt in the desert. She always explains that the winds blow the sweat; it cools her. Date palms stretch up to the stars. I know why she likes it here in this climate because I still love this desert where green is precious and rare. Where rain is a blessing worth more than gold. Yet she has not settled into her destiny. She is still wet and raw from those years of battle as a child.

I ask her, "Do you know what you are doing? Do you know the consequences?"

She lifts her head, and her chin tightens stubbornly. She always had a knack for keeping her head above the roughest of waters. She does not question me the questioner. She knows about timelessness and point of view as she is a poet.

"I have spent my life taking care of everyone else," she answers. "First it was my mother, then my brothers and sisters, and just when I thought I was going to get relief because my mother hired childcare, she took the new babysitter to work with her, and I was left with one more child to care for, the babysitter's infant son. I was nine. Then I had four children to watch instead of three through the whole summer, when everyone else was running up and down the street playing all the way to dusk. I had to stay in, watch and feed the children, clean and do laundry.

"It didn't end until I left for Indian school. Then I married as a teenager to get out of the house, had a son by him and cared for his daughter. I had no help. Then gave birth to a daughter whose

Joy Harjo

father I had to leave to save my life, and now for the first time, I have a respite. I traveled as far away from Oklahoma and New Mexico as I could with what little funds I had, all money that I made myself with no help from anyone, except for a National Endowment for the Arts grant that gave me writing time. I want my party for a while. I've earned it."

Quickly, her defiance wilted. She admitted, "I know that I made the wrong decision. The Council is always right, and I know what I should do. But that's how I feel."

The Council quietly accepted her decision. They disappeared. But not before reminding her they would return in seven years to ask again.

I wish she had said yes. I know what she will suffer. Yet she will learn. I leave her there to get on with her life.

◆　◆　◆　◆　◆

A GENEALOGY OF THE SEVEN YEAR TESTING

(There are other genealogies in play during this time. They include a genealogy of silence, a genealogy of dance, a genealogy of backward, a genealogy of race and gender, a genealogy of genealogies.)

Because she said no, there are coyotes and rogue waves and financial losses. She will be abandoned, because she abandoned herself.

She may never be offered the gift again.

The wrong answer to the question gave birth to No.

No stretched her arms and legs, secured childcare, and found her way to a disco.

She was a dancer like her mother and father. She danced to oblivion. Oblivion is a real place. There's even a disco ball.

As for spiritual and physical bankruptcy,

No signed on the line.

No lost a job. There was another. No reported:

My first week in the English Department of my first tenure-track teaching job in Boulder, Colorado, a senior colleague walked into my office without asking my permission, sat on my desk, recounted the biblical Jacob and Esau story. He told me I was akin to Esau's untaught wildness. He, on the other hand, was civilized, and a Jacob poet. I did not counter his argument. Maybe he was right.

No continued to be a primitive poet acting out her primitive ways. She was not into writing poetry as a means of proving intellectual superiority or to show off her knowledge of Greek classical mythologies.

Her poems were rejected by magazines. Maybe because they were primitive. Her first books were published with few reviews.

John Lennon was killed.

And there was the jealousy of No's competitors:

"You are only here as a poet because of your looks, your
femaleness or you fill the Native quota: only one allowed."
"No, you have children and your poetry."
"No man likes a woman who writes better than him, etc."

And the takedowns and discouragements

No liked a spoon for an edge, a lift.
Smoking it took her higher
but had the potential
to eat too much into the grocery bill.

No, said no.
She preferred how her spirit could travel
in prayer
like poetry
without the false realms
made by manufacturers of highs.

No learned to take responsibility.

No stood up for justice though she didn't stand up for herself.

No lost her son when he went looking for his father—
that boy could sing; he could draw anything.
He went to Indian school and helped the beauty queen climb in
the window
to safety, washed her clothes and made her breakfast.

That's my son.

There is no place for the hurt of letting go to live, to live.

Blow it.

No's daughter took it all in as she floated on clouds
that brought rain to the desert.
What power in her hands of thunderbolts—
it rained and rained until the dawn.

And butterflies flew out, every color, No exclaimed
as they flew around her daughter, the baby and her.
Her daughter would use all those colors in her art.

That's my girl.

No flew past the southern border to witness for justice. She
watched the same story there. Colonization rolled over the earth,
destroying environment, cultures, and children.

No had no place to put the story of Amazonian settlers hunting
Indians.

No studied the spiritual texts of Coltrane and Davis. She listened
nightly in jazz clubs in a city that lived on the shoulder of the
mountain god.

One day No picked up a saxophone. The notes, like words,
helped her begin to find the way back.

Her father died and she took care of his body, his spirit, with her
daughter by her side.

Joy Harjo

Part of her had to die so she could be born again as herself.

She heard Weather Report in concert.

No roamed for seven years, dragging her roots behind her.

She grew tired of the party. This was after the first day.

She could hear the call for "*locv, locv*" though she was far away
in miles and time.

What a spectacle as from the roots that dragged behind her grew
a pine wood forest in which lived a white deer who attended
to her dreams. There was a home constructed for the children
to come home, for the grandchildren. There was a desk with a
typewriter. The typewriter became a computer. In the corner was
a saxophone. And there was a huge table at the center stacked
with books, music, and food. There were woods to run in.

No knocked on the door of the little house in the pine forest. At
first no one answered. And then a little girl peeked out, her first
granddaughter, who told her she was about to be born to her
daughter.

No returned to the desert seven years later, after she had left,
to welcome this girl who would be born there. The Council
welcomed her home from her sojourn.

No turned in the direction of becoming with her grandchildren
beginning to surround her.

There is no story, No told them, without the hard parts.

The hard parts teach us how to live, so we will know without a doubt what we carry.

Yes, she replied when they asked again, when they returned Seven years later. No became yes.

◆　◆　◆　◆　◆

Poet Warrior gave birth to two children
And acquired more children along the way
Through association, marriage, and love.
Those children gave birth to children
There were more and more story bringers
In her world.
They became her fiercest teachers
Of how there is no end to love
And of how it plants itself
Deeper than earth
Or sky.

◆　◆　◆　◆　◆

WITHOUT WARNING MY DAUGHTER, I drove up to the Indian boarding school in Gallup, New Mexico, to get her. I hadn't told her I was coming. I had been concerned about her being so far away. Her voice on our phone calls was sounding distant and troubled. I was worried at what she wasn't saying. It was a several-hour drive north from my teaching job in Tucson. I got a substitute for my classes and left for the winding highways through forests

Joy Harjo

and mesas. I did not tell her I was coming to bring her home. I had a sense she might flee. She didn't believe she was anything like me, but like me, she would do anything for love. She will endure and she will fight.

She was in love with a young man who was a mathematical genius. When he was accused of cheating by teachers for his high scores on math tests, because they didn't believe a Navajo kid could be that smart, he walked out of high school. He moved back home with his family and went to work as a sacker for a supermarket. Between the time of my daughter's friends spotting my car arriving in the parking lot of the administration office and me signing the papers to release her back into my care, she had called her boyfriend and he had sped over on his motorcycle and picked her up.

In shock, I gathered up my daughter's few belongings from her dorm room. Then I went to look for her.

That night I searched the streets of that dusty border town for hours alone in my car. My beautiful daughter was somewhere in this town, an Indian border town notorious for maltreatment of Indian people. I searched every backstreet and imagined finding her in a garage, the trunk of a car, in a backroom of a trafficker or anyplace else my imagination could go. I looked and looked as night fell and took over. I despaired. I did not find her or her boyfriend, another teen refugee from parental concern. Historical trauma ran through every bloodline that defined them.

That night I stayed in a rundown hotel on Route 66. In the heyday of the highway this hotel had harbored movie stars of cowboy westerns. Their movie stills lined the hallways. That night was one of the toughest in my world. I could not find my daughter. I did not know where she was and there was no one to call to help. My daughter's father was unreachable. I had to return to my job and leave her there in that hell. She didn't want to be found.

Within a month, after working with my daughter's boy-friend's family and his counselor at the Indian hospital we located them, and a meeting was brokered in his counselor's office with his sister as a go-between. When my baby came walking in from the street, battle-worn and hungry, I saw on her face she was pregnant. There was no way I was going to walk out of there without her even if that meant bringing her boyfriend with us. As unconventional as that was, that's what I had to do, for fierce love.

I knew that if I had brought my daughter without him, she would have run away into the dark to return to him. She would have crossed dangerous miles and highways alone, a much farther distance than from one end of a border town to the other. (However, a border town can be hundreds of emotional miles, from one block to the next.)

♦ ♦ ♦ ♦ ♦

WHAT I DIDN'T COUNT ON is how much I would come to love the young man I reluctantly brought home that afternoon with my daughter, for whom I signed on legally to serve as guardian. I still keep his long-expired guardianship papers tucked into my important paper file.

My granddaughter was born a little over eight months later. There is no way to communicate what it is like to be at the birthing of your daughter's first child, a granddaughter merging into a matriarchal continuum. That was one of the best days. It will always be one of the best days.

Now, breathe.
And when you breathe remember the source of the gift of all
    breathing.

When you walk, remember the source of the gift of all walking.
And when you run, remember the source of the gift of all
    running.
And when you laugh, remember the source of the gift of all
    laughter.
And when you cry, remember the source of the gift of all tears.
And when your heart is broken, remember the source of the gift
    of all breaking.
And when your heart is put back together, remember the source
    of all putting back together.

❖ ❖ ❖ ❖ ❖

I CAME TO KNOW THIS young man during that time of pregnancy, birth, and caretaking. He worked hard flipping burgers daily at a local McDonald's. The same kind of mind that can generate and understand complex mathematical equations and configurations also carries the ability for music, for interdimensional geometrics. We spent many evenings talking about what matters, how it matters, and the impossibility of what is possible. For my birthday that year he and my daughter sacrificed to buy me a pair of diamond stud earrings. I saw each tiny diamond as a representation of the light within each of them, a light that shone with an intent to live a meaningful life.

I learned he was haunted. Some nights were not easy. He would pace. He had difficult dreams. He told me that because his father had shot a girlfriend he caught with a lover, then had shot and killed himself (the girlfriend lived), he was doomed to carry out that violence. It was in him. My daughter and I tried to talk him through the story in a way that would lead him to healing, reminding him there was medicine for this. There were ceremonies that could relieve him of this burden. I remember him shaking his head telling us that nothing could help.

He loved his daughter with his same deep dark eyes. She inherited many of his gifts, which included a perceptive sensitivity. He loved my daughter, who wanted him to know that he was loved no matter what had happened to him. He grew to respect and love me. We made a family. We moved from Arizona back to New Mexico for my new job. They found their own place. My daughter attended a high school for teenage mothers.

One day in the middle of nothing related, just a rambling thought pattern, I saw what was going to happen. The darkness that followed this gifted young man was going to overtake him, just as he predicted. What had been planted in him by the violent loss of his father was calling it. Though he loved my daughter, he was going to try to kill her. It wouldn't be him killing her, rather it would be the guilt and grief passed down from the young man's father that had taken hold. It was as he had kept telling me. It was there and he hadn't been able to shake it off. It had taken him down and would try and take my daughter, the same as it had overtaken his father.

I met my daughter at her school for lunch one day and told her what I saw. I told her that her life was in danger. I pleaded for her to save herself. She asserted that she knew her life better than I would ever know it. She held herself proudly and apart from me.

I begged. I remember how blue the sky was, how it contrasted with the despair I was feeling over what felt certain to happen. I was begging for her life with the same kind of fierceness that had driven her for love into the streets of a border town. I tried to reason with her.

"What if it were your daughter who was about to walk off a cliff to her death? You would do anything to protect her."

She said nothing as she let herself out of the car. My presence was overwhelming to her and she wanted to make her own way, her own decisions.

They moved to Gallup to a trailer home his mother acquired to house them. One morning he held a knife to my daughter, forced her into the car and drove her out of town to kill her. As they drove out to the killing, she convinced him that he would need money to get away because the police would come looking for him. Just take me to an ATM and I will get you some cash, I remember her telling me she had told him. When they drove up, she jumped out and ran for safety.

She finished her semester of school and kept moving forward with her life. She found a new relationship. Her baby's father worked jobs intermittently, then fell into a life on the streets. He was still shadowed and was troubled about the loss of my daughter and my granddaughter. As the years went on, it was my daughter he turned to for help as he roamed the streets alone. She found coats and blankets for him for winter. She loves fiercely and without end. Her love is brave beyond brave.

The last time I saw him was at his daughter's high school graduation party. He stood stiffly apart from everyone. It was difficult for him to be there, yet he showed up. I spoke to him for a while. I argued still, there is a way out of this. You don't have to live this way. But he would not see to let his burden go.

Within a few years of his daughter's college graduation four years later, he was run down by a car in the streets of Albuquerque by a white man angered because he was sick of all these Indians. His body was dragged seven hundred feet and he was killed. Witnesses called it a hate crime, though the driver was never punished.

* * * * *

I HAD TO LET THE tears turn to dew glistening at dawn on
small green plants emerging from the desert sand to make food.

* * * * *

ADAPTED FROM THE MEMORIAL SERVICE:

I knew their sacrifice. Those diamond lights were two children,
Making their way through the suffering
Of our families, our peoples.
When the baby was born, the whole family came together to
     welcome her.
She is evidence of this diamond kind of love,
the love of the sky and earth for us.
He would look at his baby, then my daughter, then me, and say:
"All of you look so much alike."
He'd shake his head, a big smile on his face.
We all loved that smile.
Yet sadness would not leave him.
There's historical trauma we all carry.
Some of us carry a heavier part of the burden,
So that the rest of the family doesn't suffer as much—
That's what he did.
We do not always understand.
Nor will we have the complete story until we are beyond earth.
We are a love larger than any disappointment
Any difficulty, or missteps, or accidents.
Within the arms of that Creator there is never judgment

Only care and concern, no matter who we are or
What we have done or are doing on our path here.
Love cannot be broken.
There are some things that take more than an eternity
To understand.

Part Five

TEACHERS

* * * * *

EVERYONE IS A TEACHER. YOU are a teacher to someone else.
These are my teachers: these poems and songs, these poets and
musicians, these relatives and those who stand against as enemies
to test. These are my teachers: these healers, these healed and broken. I have stood and I have fallen in this story field. I have chased
an attacker who was killing a gay man, through the streets of New
York City, have read poetry in the coffee plantations of Central
America with Claribel Alegría, even as I have found my legs to
stand after a rape. The Pacific Ocean is one of my most beloved
teachers. The fire at the ceremonial grounds is another. My mother's and father's death teachings were some of the most profound.
The best teachers are exacting. There is no end to learning.

* * * * *

The Old Ones always knew where to find Poet Warrior
As she roamed and moved from city to city.
She had been born into a restless society
Of immigrants whose roots led to Europe
Asia and Africa, always looking for home.
Our indigenous nations were transformed by
Governments and corporations
For gold, oil, and coal—some of us kept running
Until we could not be found.
Until we could not even find ourselves.
Poet Warrior began to forget who she was in the clatter
Of the multicorporate glut.
To remind her, they brought her teachers.

* * * * *

AS I CHILD, I COULD go into any grassy area and find a grass
or garter snake playmate. I'd play with them for a while, walking
with them in my pocket, on my arm, scaring others with them.
Then I'd let them go. They sometimes let me find them again.

Yesterday I was walking to put bags of wild onions in my car
and almost stepped on a smooth green snake. We both jumped
back in surprise and for protection. We stopped to observe each
other. I hadn't seen a snake in a few years, and don't come across
them very often these days. To see "Smooth Green Snake" gave
me happiness, a green happiness.

Seeing snakes doesn't always evoke such a response, especially
if it's a snake curled up to strike, rattling its warning. Snakes slide

Smooth green snake

Joy Harjo

along the earth mysteriously, in long narrow bodies, usually mind-ing their own business. They know what we don't know, what can be gleaned from the underneath of human consciousness.

A snake can be a messenger, and the message can be either ominous or friendly. Or there may be no message at all. The snake could be just passing by, like the car in the next lane. The last snake warning I witnessed came from a long dark snake who swiveled under our car parked in front of our condo a few years ago. We were curious, bent down to see it, and it swiftly slithered up the decorative stone outcropping along the side of the building. It was about three feet long. I didn't have a foreboding, but I made a note of its unusual presence. The next afternoon, as we drove in the same car, the one we had found the snake under, a driver tried to run us off the road for several miles on the interstate, forcing us into the median wall. We eventually made it safely to our exit. That was the message of the snake. I still wonder who sent it, as the snake would have had no reason on its own to come find us; or maybe it's not that at all. Maybe we trespassed on the snake's territory, offended it in some manner unknown to us.

In many cultures snakes represent enemies, difficulties, sexu-ality, or danger. In the Judeo-Christian origin story, a snake fig-ures prominently as a demonic tempter of a woman who, because she listens and eats an apple offered by the snake, is responsible for the loss of paradise, for the demotion of women to slave status. I question the reasoning behind a cultural pantheon that includes no female power figures in the leadership circle, when the natural world shows us that no life is created without male and female power joined together.

In my experience, snakes and their character and intent are quite diverse, as with other living earth beings. Humans do not have dominion over them. They have their own dominions and consciousness. I have encountered snakes both in the physical and in dreamtime. Sometimes they signal an enemy. I know this because of the way they move and how they are thinking. There is a sense about them that reads "enemy." We usually know when someone doesn't mean us well. You will feel it in your gut, or as we say in the Mvskoke language, *poyvfekcv*. That is where the spirit or the knowing lives.

We know that rattlesnake, water moccasin, and cottonmouth bites are dangerous. It is their protection. And most don't kill ruthlessly, though, as with any people, there can be a few rogue beings who cross moral and ethical lines for sport killing.

I remember the story of the gang of rogue male elephants in Africa who roamed the lands killing just to kill. This was unusual behavior for elephants. This gang had been raised without fathers. Someone who recognized this corralled them with an elder male elephant who taught them. When they were let loose again into elephant society, the desire to sport kill had left them. They now had understanding. They had guidance that gave them a sense of family.

Some snakes are helper snakes. They give guidance and messages. A Tie-Snake lives in a dangerous place of changing currents in the Chattanooga River. They also live at the bottom of lakes and ponds. They are powerful, transformational beings. We respect them.

Once I was walking along in a dream. I felt someone tugging at my pants leg. I looked down to see a snake. The snake lifted up to speak with me. He was very friendly. I felt no fear at his presence, just curiosity for what he had to say.

"I have a message," said the snake. "It's for Leslie Silko."

This did not surprise me, because Leslie often surfaces in my dreamtime. We catch up there when we haven't seen each other in person for a time.

Joy Harjo

"Please tell her . . ." The snake messenger gave me information that made no sense to me, but I promised to pass it along.

When I told her, Leslie replied that the message was exactly what she needed for the painting she was working on that honored this snake's people.

When it comes to snakes, or anyone else sliding, swimming, or walking in this world, we can usually read intent, though we may let cultural misunderstandings mar awareness. I've learned in all my years of living and traveling the world that most people in this world mean no intentional harm, be they two-legged, four-legged, winged, or finned. But when they do, pay attention. You will know who they are by the signs.

◆ ◆ ◆ ◆ ◆

THE NOVELIST, POET, AND ACTIVIST Meridel Le Sueur, a child of the Midwest, became one of my earliest mentors. I was an undergraduate student at the University of New Mexico when I attended a private gathering of local women held in honor of her visit. I was introduced to Meridel as an up-and-coming poet. We must have exchanged addresses because after that initial meeting we began a correspondence that continued until her death. In those times we wrote letters. Or we called and spoke on the telephone. I must have given her a copy of my first book, a chapbook called *The Last Song*, which prompted her first letter.

As I came to know Meridel through her letters and by reading those of her novels and poetry that were in print, I learned that she had been blacklisted, and that her writings had essentially disappeared from American letters. I learned how she had been stalked by the FBI for years in the 1940s and '50s and had been kept from working because she was a member of the Communist Party. Until then, she had been a well-known writer and poet, published by major presses. When she was targeted during the McCarthy era, it was unlawful to publish her writings; and any employer or potential employer was threatened. She told me that even when she took work in childcare the FBI would show up at the place of work and she would lose her job. It was difficult to get by, especially with two young daughters to support. She wrote about the Depression, about breadlines, about the lives of the poor and women and others whose voices were left out of the American story. The feminists rediscovered her in the early '70s and began to reprint and publish her writings, which ranged from novels to poetry to children's books.

Le Sueur's novel *The Girl* is a tightly rendered tale given shape by the stories she gathered from women during the Depression who struggled to find work and feed their children. Martin Scorsese optioned it and I was in line to write the screenplay, but like most optioned film projects it was never produced.

One of my favorite moments in my long friendship with her was the day she arrived in Iowa City by bus. I had found funds as a student at the University of Iowa to bring her to read and speak. Her fiction and poetry were not generally included in the curriculum, though many of her writings were classic texts, and she was highly experimental in her use of time and narrative. My children and I picked her up at the bus station. She carried tote bags on her arms with gifts of books for the children and me, and a Mason jar of tequila she had sipped discreetly from as she traveled from St. Paul. No one would suspect a kind old lady of illegally drinking on the bus.

One of her classic poems is the epic *The Dread Road*, which tells of a hellish bus trip from Albuquerque north to Colorado, the central figure being a woman rider who clutches her dead child wrapped in a blanket in her arms. They drive through treacherous history, through the killing of striking mine laborers by the U.S. government. The woman rider had no funds for healthcare.

Meridel's bus trip to see in us in Iowa was different. My literary grandmother made friends and probably helped them out, even shared her tequila. Once when I had no money as I was cobbling together a living by freelancing and a performance now and then and was wondering how I was going to feed my children, a hundred-dollar bill arrived in the mail, wrapped in a letter from her. I hadn't said anything to her about my need. Her intuitive kindness saved us.

Another lit memory: we are in Santa Fe and a circle of women admirers have propped Meridel up in a corner with a good view of the dance floor. Though she was no longer able to stand sturdily, she loved dance. When she was a young woman she went to Hollywood and was picked to be in silent films as an actress and dancer. She was thrilled to be included in the dance party with a group of young writers and poets.

She looked after me with admonitions in her letters. She'd warn me to beware of popularity. You cannot stake a life based on fleeting standards set by a fickle populace. She told me not to be dismayed in situations where I present and speak and am disregarded because men do not listen to female voices.

I saw how this happened at a conference I attended with her in the Midwest, organized by the men with whom she had worked side-by-side as a cultural worker through the years. She was the only woman on the panel that morning, a female sage among men who would prove that they did not listen to women.

Though Meridel spoke powerfully, more as a seer of history than a suit of tradition, it was as she said: the men on the panel looked away when she spoke and did not directly acknowledge her.

I was upset afterward about their disregard for her. She reminded me that we have to believe in ourselves. We cannot expect men to want to listen as they are used to listening only to themselves. In her time, women did not occupy this kind of public space, but in my generation, women would.

She called me to tell me she was dying. I stood in the kitchen of that tall, drafty rental house in Santa Fe, always full of dust no matter how much sweeping. I recall holding the receiver next to my ear, dinner on the stove and my daughter and her friend playing in the other room. She was old enough that dying seemed the natural course of events; still, even if your mother, father, relative, partner or friend is over a hundred years old, the leaving means they are going from you, and their disappearance will make a hole in your earth story.

Tears began gathering in my lungs. I did not want to lose my wise mentor. However, my grief soon turned to curiosity when I realized she was ecstatic about the journey.

"I am dying!" she proclaimed. This dying was just like any other road. It was unknown territory, mysterious and compelling. Her body would disintegrate to reveal yet another story. She reveled in the unfolding, as if her body were hills and mountains being slowly changed by the sun, by rain and time.

Within a few weeks I received a box of some of her most beloved belongings. She sent me a red wool powwow shawl with the American Indian Movement logo on it. She sent me a necklace of a thick strand of turquoise, another of amber.

I assumed her death was imminent. But Meridel didn't die until nearly fifteen years later, at the age of ninety-six. She had then gone to live with her daughter Rachel and her family not far from the Mississippi River just over the bridge to Wisconsin. When her daughter found her, Meridel's head was resting on her arms on her writing table. Her pen was in her hand. She had been hard at work on three "nounless" novels.

◆　◆　◆　◆　◆

THIS WITH MY LAST BREATH

written by Meridel Le Sueur, November 13–14, 1996

November—Thanksgiving
Nov 13–14
This is like adolescence—all your body is
changing . . . the glands . . . the center glandular
shift . . . fast changes.
substance tempo another kind of sleep . . .
my reality seems different . . . I am a stranger to myself . . .
    where are these alien feelings coming from?
        O come to me . . . I am entertaining
some other person and nothing is familiar to me.
        It's not sleep . . . I am simply gone . . .
entirely gone from memory of the body and also
as if some dramatic character has
fallen from you and left you amazed alone
without your personality. Yes
you have died . . . that traditional person
and all her memories and took on alien
memories.
    It is strange you are taking
on a new personality . . .
a stranger . . . alienated . . . unfamiliar.

I write differently . . .
Then I seem to be gone
My body inhibits . . . immobile . . .
an empty house. I am sitting here as no one
absolutely no one. The wind blowing
into your valves and caves and habitat.
Then another tide sweeps on all
the fire and identity of a powerful woman
of entire circulation. All the floods sing and
breaking new force and tide
and no need to do anything.
We've taken off our persona and
removed a dress to make a study of bones.
The death of the decorative person
comes back. Call back the naked and the reality.
We're shedding . . . what chickens do to
shed your feathers. Molt. Change your reality.
But this shedding of all your
costume and personature is most amazing . . .
a certain clothing of personalities falls
away leaving you naked . . . bare.
Death of a shallow person.
Return to depth.
Death
Who is that with you?
It is one big movement . . . bring
the heart the blood flow in her river . . .
new return. In a movement from many
keening coming.
He comes now the night is ripening.
Yes. All up and down the great cottonwoods.

Joy Harjo

30 million died . . .
   Trees of opulence.
   September   1996
   Girl   Girl
Behind being woman
Broken in the fragment of a stolen
nation . . . psychic notion. In the Indian world . . .
Indian earth a people on the earth.
Sound and resonance of earth . . . memory
Mind and flesh. Human mind flesh . . .
Carrying the print. Racial memory. Speak.
Communal culture   speak
O speak.   O speak.   O speak.
Liken centuries to give the dream and
   the people.
   New Crop
   New Pace.
   Mind and dream. The racial
memory . . . build the body and mind the
memory the song.
   What is there to be given. Like
insanity the pall of the directed . . . the
ghostly.
It builds. The death builds.
   The flesh is charged. Memory is present.
   It is a substance. Slow down.
Slow fragments print with the body.
   . . . a certain expectation. Star built memory.
It is slow.
   What is real.
   What builds.

What grows form.
What is fantastic . . . created.
What is real.

❖   ❖   ❖   ❖   ❖

I THOUGHT I WOULD DREAM about Meridel, or that she would
otherwise make herself known to me. It made sense that she didn't
return immediately to this realm. She had already embraced the
next story, a place in which none of our nouns could go with us.
Then once when I was thinking I should give up writing because I
was turned down by publishers and no one else seemed to care or
have any interest in what I was writing, I had a dream.

I was in bed with an illness. Meridel stood over me singing
and praying, with a shell of smoke in her hands, cleaning my
spirit. When I awoke the next morning from the dream, I put one
foot in front of the other, one word in front of the next.

I never saw Meridel Le Sueur again in dreams or otherwise,
but I feel her moving within my story as I approach the platform
where she left, to take a place next to her.

❖   ❖   ❖   ❖   ❖

I WAS A YOUNG POET attending the Great Midwestern Book-
show in Minneapolis, probably one of the largest book fairs in the
country in the early eighties. So many poetry gods and goddesses
were speaking and giving readings that it was hard to figure out
where to go listen next. I squeezed into a place on the floor of a
large, packed room to hear the poet Audre Lorde. I appreciated
the way she dressed contemporary African traditional with her
hair wrapped in a colorful kente cloth.

I had been using her poems as maps, the way some of our indigenous peoples used songs for star maps. They told me how to get from here to there, in a land of beautiful diversity as it existed within the perverted reality of racial and gender hate. It can be a tricky landscape, even trickier for women. I was thrilled that I was hearing Audre Lorde read for the first time.

To hear poetry in person is to experience poetry as it is traditionally meant to be experienced, that is, you feel it breathe and experience how it travels out dynamically to become part of the winds skirting the earth, even as we inhale and take the words into our bloodstream. To speak is to bring into being. Poetry can bring rain, make someone fall in love, can hold the grief of a nation. Poetry is essentially an oral art whose roots are intertwined with music and dance.

Each poem of Audre's was a rendering in intimate and personal references toward the notion that what is intimate and personal has political import. Her manner of reading welcomed everyone into a circle. She told me once that when she wrote, she imagined a circle of woman around a fire. She would speak, listening for words to make change, to draw people closer together to investigate what they had in common, as well as their differences. She was ushering in a post–Civil Rights changed world, one in which all people were empowered, one in which we could speak across differences, one in which she could speak directly of forbidden love.

One cold winter day when I was far from home, where it reached eighty below windchill factor and we'd still have classes, I browsed in the university bookstore. That's where I found Audre. I pulled her poetry book *Coal* off the shelf and stood there in the bookstore and read it through. I could not leave it there because I needed it to keep me warm in that far-away place, a place where my voice felt as frozen as the Iowa River iced up for the winter. Audre Lorde's poetry became a fire keeping my spirit alert with warmth.

After she read the poem "Love Poem," I anonymously called out from the audience, "Read it again." I had never been so brave as to speak out in an audience, but I also had never experienced such bravery in a poet. Her bravery inspired mine. I had not heard a poem so blatantly sensual since the "Song of Solomon" in the Bible.

> *Speak earth and bless me with what is richest*
> *make sky flow honey out of my hips*
> *rigid as mountains*
> *spread over a valley*
> *carved out by the mouth of rain.*

However, my favorite poem of hers remains "Litany for Survival." It was the ember for many of my poems, including the poem "I Give You Back" or what has become known as the "Fear Poem."

A LITANY FOR SURVIVAL

For those of us who live at the shoreline
standing upon the constant edges of decision
crucial and alone
for those of us who cannot indulge
the passing dreams of choice
who love in the doorways coming and going
in the hours between dawns
looking inward and outward
at once before and after

seeking a now that can breed
futures
like bread in our children's mouths
so their dreams will not reflect
the death of ours:

For those of us
who were imprinted with fear
like a faint line in the center of our foreheads
learning to be afraid with our mother's milk
for by this weapon
this illusion of some safety to be found
the heavy-footed hoped to silence us
For all of us
this instant and this triumph
we were never meant to survive.

And when the sun rises we are afraid
it might remain
when the sun sets we are afraid
it might not rise in the morning
when our stomachs are full we are afraid
of indigestion
when our stomachs are empty we are afraid
we may never eat again
when we are loved we are afraid
love will vanish
when we are alone we are afraid
love will never return
and when we speak we are afraid
our words will not be heard

nor welcomed
but when we are silent
we are still afraid

So it is better to speak
remembering
we were never meant to survive

At the end of her reading, I was emboldened and approached her to speak, one of many in a line of admirers. She invited me.

"Let's find a place to sit and break bread together."

As we sat together in the crowded cafeteria, I worked up courage to ask her, in so many words, what it felt like to know what she knew, and I asked her, but I don't remember with what words, had she figured it all out, this poetry, this life?

She threw her head back and laughed. "Noooooooo, honey."

After that we became friends.

She taught me that there is no separation between being a poet and being a mother and a lover. All are warrior roles. Audre Lorde's wisdom songs folded into the consciousness of my poetry. They tell me to this day that there is no end to the quest for justice, for knowledge, and remind me to make poems to hold everything that slips past the failure of memory, of love.

◆ ◆ ◆ ◆ ◆

THOUGH I LOVED POETRY ALL of my life, it wasn't until poems like "The Delight Song of Tsoai-Talee" by N. Scott Momaday that I turned to the making of poetry. Like Momaday, I came to poetry as an artist who painted and drew. And both Momaday and I have a love of those traditional rituals that place the speaker/

singer into an intimate relationship with a place on earth, a people. I believe every poem is ritual: there is a naming, a beginning, a knot or question, then possibly revelation, and then closure, which can be opening, setting the reader, speaker, or singer out and back on a journey. I can hear the tribal speaker in his voice, in whatever mode of performance. And when I trust my voice to go where it needs to be, to find home, it returns to where it belongs, back to the source of its longing.

My voice returns to the sound of the voices of those way back who made an imprint on this earth. I hear the Arkansas River and how the waters flow east to our homelands. I hear my father's cousin from Okemah, the barrel racer Dona Jo Harjo—we always reminded each other of how we both sounded like our beloved aunt Lois Harjo. We inherited her voice, which was as deep and wide as the river home. When I write, those old voices inspire me, and surprise me with what they know. Maybe that's how most wisdom works. Sometimes it can be corralled into print, in languages in books, but it lives more abundantly when spoken and welcomes a place to live on earth.

◆　◆　◆　◆　◆

WE CAN CALL CULTURE BACK. I am reminded of a Sugpiaq story, told to me by a Sugpiaq anthropologist, Sven Haakanson, who specializes in documenting and preserving the culture and language of his people. Years ago, as he was coming up, the people were in crisis. Their culture was nearly gone. There were no new native speakers being taught, and fewer culture-bearers. The people began by taking their language and cultural knowledge back, sometimes one piece at a time. They soon discovered that it had always been there, hidden. It hadn't died, rather it existed silently as a living being in collections scattered across the world. It was lonely and, like all living beings, once reawaked it began to thrive with attention and nurturing.

Years before, during the worst of it, Russian fur traders lined up Sugpiat people and shot musket balls through them, to see how many people could be killed with one shot. When the children were torn from their parents' arms and held as hostages, one Tlingit man, who loved a Sugpiat woman, learned their songs and taught them to singers from his village, keeping the songs alive, to be gifted back when they would emerge from this destruction. Recently the Sugpiat songs were returned home by the Tlingit. There were many tears that day as Tlingit people sang the songs back to the Sugpiat people nearly a century later, as the Sugpiat received the songs that they had thought were gone. The songs never died. They were living within Tlingit Nation, because of love, waiting to be gifted back to the Sugpiat Nation to sing again.

✦ ✦ ✦ ✦ ✦

EVERY POEM HAS ANCESTORS. KIOWA singers and orators can be found staking words to the ground, with poetic lines appearing as prayer flags waving in the winds in Momaday's poem "The Delight Song of Tsoai-Talee." I can also hear the long-legged poetry of Walt Whitman, who is considered one of the original American poetry ancestors. I wonder who influenced Walt Whitman to release poetry from the highly stylized European forms, to make a poetry that flowed like the winds rippling over vast fields of leaves of grass.

Whitman had quite the interest in American Indians. His life was framed by the Trails of Tears banishments of tribal nations from the East to the West. The Wounded Knee Massacre occurred near the end of his life. In the first edition of *Leaves of Grass*, published in 1855, American Indians/Natives appear in five of the twelve poems. Whitman was the only American poet known to have worked in the Indian Bureau of the Department of the Interior, where he met and conversed with Native delegations of tribal nations. It appears, then, that he might have been somewhat familiar with Native oratorical skills, and with the craft apparent in those skills that informs poetry. The Library of Congress holds an original draft of his poem "Osceola," in which he recounts the death of the Seminole leader by that name. Early in his writing career Whitman also wrote a novella, *The Half-Breed: A Tale of the Western Frontier*. It's time that Native nations' early influences in American poetry be recognized.

Yet Whitman, like others of his age, though he was sympathetic with the "plight" of the country's indigenous peoples, agreed that American Indians were at the root savages in need of what civilization could offer.

Momaday's poem, and perhaps every poem, establishes itself as a kind of "I am" assertion. A poem exists because it says: "I am the voice of the poet or what is moving through time, place, and event; I am sound sense and words; I am made of all this; and though I may not know where I am going, I will show you, and we will sing together."

Like Whitman, like the Kiowa people long before the establishment of what is now called the United States, Momaday's poem establishes that no matter who we are on this earth, we embody everything, we are related to all life, all beings. This assertion appears at the opening of nearly every ritual gathering in indigenous lands and cultures. We stand at the center of the circle that the poem has established with words and images, and as we do, we are in good relation, and alive.

In this time of a virus roaming methodically across the earth, infecting the earth's population, this poem centers us in the natural world, and declares a healing. I imagine the voice of Earth speaking the first stanza. The Earth, and all beings, are always moving toward healing. This poem reminds us.

THE DELIGHT SONG OF TSOAI-TALEE

I am a feather on the bright sky
I am the blue horse that runs in the plain
I am the fish that rolls, shining, in the water
I am the shadow that follows a child
I am the evening light, the lustre of meadows
I am an eagle playing with the wind
I am a cluster of bright beads
I am the farthest star
I am the cold of dawn
I am the roaring of the rain
I am the glitter on the crust of the snow
I am the long track of the moon in a lake
I am a flame of four colors
I am a deer standing away in the dusk
I am a field of sumac and the pomme blanche
I am an angle of geese in the winter sky
I am the hunger of a young wolf
I am the whole dream of these things

You see, I am alive, I am alive
I stand in good relation to the earth

Joy Harjo

I stand in good relation to the gods
I stand in good relation to all that is beautiful
I stand in good relation to the daughter of Tsen-tainte
You see, I am alive, I am alive

Every poem has poetry ancestors. My poetry would not exist without Audre Lorde's "Litany for Survival," without Mvskoke stomp dance call-and-response, without Adrienne Rich's "Diving into the Wreck," without Meridel Le Sueur or N. Scott Momaday, without death or sunrise, without Walt Whitman, or Navajo horse songs, or Langston Hughes, without rain, without grief, without—

◆　◆　◆　◆　◆

Poet Warrior found a job in Los Angeles.
She lived where the Hollywood sign branded the city.
And there were doughnut houses everywhere.
Glitter, glitter of broken glass and desperate money—
Orange blossoms sweetened the air.
She went to work with Story Warrior.
They were like twins, given birth to by a mother—
she loved the talk of gods.
In that shifting time there was much danger,
isn't that when things tend to happen?
Giants are born, anyone could be swallowed by the monster.

One day they saw the changing of the worlds.
They ran with tender blessings into the streets.
They carried sharpened arrows
and the promise of fathers who were strangers.

They went to school, worked jobs at the factory,
learned to buy everything they needed.
They forgot the smell and warning of the monster
and the reason for the journey.

The sun zigzagged across this land to watch them.
Most humans breathed and died without knowing they breathed
    planets.
It's easy to get sidetracked, and difficult to see farther
than these skin houses we walk this earth in.

Humans were created by mistake.
Someone laughed and we came crawling out.
That was the beginning of the drama;
we were hooked then.
What a wild dilemma,
how to make it to the stars on a highway slick with fear.

One night they stared at the glittering dark for clues,
for anything to sing to shine,
convinced someone had forgotten them.
In the whirlpool of the city the monster found them,
walking in the glamour without their arrows.
It was two young boys who could have been their brothers.
They held them up said they would kill them.

They wanted to kill the monster,
so it would not destroy the earth and take it with him,
or erase the dreams of humans in the ordinary world.
They gave the boys their money in the whirling wake of violence.

Joy Harjo

They, too, wanted to love but did not know how to say it.

The spirit of the story could smell the danger.
Climbed down the clouds
because things had gone too far.
It breathed in life from all directions.
The running boys were in the beautiful pattern.
They followed.

Humans were created by mistake.
Someone laughed and we came crawling out.
That was the beginning of the drama;
we were hooked then. What a wild dilemma,
how to make it to the stars on a highway slick with fear.

❖　❖　❖　❖　❖

WHEN MY THIRD GRANDDAUGHTER'S BODY was forming,
I watched and listened to what was going on in the atmosphere,
to give a clue about this spirit, what she would need once she
arrived here to take on her part of the story. I wanted to make a
kind of map.

The spirit plays about the mother and father during development and can enter and leave the forming physical body at will.
We are each very individual, even in this matter. Some lodge in the
body for most of the pregnancy, others fly in at first breath. This
is a very vulnerable time for the pregnant mother, the expecting
father, and the whole family, as the earth house is being built.
What is said or done around the mother and the family can have a
deleterious or positive effect on the forming child. Sing songs that

inspire. Learn something useful. Do not fight. Don't hang around with angry people. Protect the baby with prayer and good will.

As I listened, a powerful story was making the rounds in the Native community. There was a Navajo woman who lived far out on the reservation in a *hogan*, the traditional home of the indigenous people there. She was of a righteous nature, still prayed in the morning with cornmeal, took care of her sheep, and was loved and well-respected by her neighbors. She was also blind. She was visited one day by the Holy Ones. As her *hogan* filled with the powerful presence of sacredness, the Holy Ones told her, as they towered over her, that they came to give a warning to the people.

We are nearing times where we will experience earth changes, famine, and strife, because people are forgetting their original teachings.

The Holy Ones instructed her to tell everyone to keep hold of their traditional ways, to remember prayer and to care for each other, for all living things, for this earth, or they will suffer.

I knew that my granddaughter was bringing in special gifts that would assist with these times we are moving into, times in which we are reckoning with our lack of respect and attention to what matters in this place named Earth in English, or *Ekvnvcakv*, which is Mother Earth in Mvskoke.

I told this story at a performance with many Navajo people in attendance. Most nodded their heads in remembering. For Holy Ones to touch down in that manner is powerful and dangerous; everyone must pay attention.

Afterward, one of the women came up to me and remarked, "I saw the footprints of the Holy Ones in the sand in front of the *hogan*! They were very long and narrow."

We are in those times now. Maybe by the time you read this, we will have learned how to be human.

Joy Harjo

◆ ◆ ◆ ◆ ◆

A MAP TO THE NEXT WORLD

(for Desiray Kierra Chee)

In the last days of the fourth world, I wished to make a map for
those who would climb through the hole in the sky.

My only tools were the desires of humans as they emerged from
the killing fields, from the bedrooms and the kitchens.

For the soul is a wanderer with many hands and feet.

The map must be of sand and can't be read by ordinary light.
It must carry fire to the next tribal town, for renewal of spirit.

In the legend are instructions on the language of the land,
how it was we forgot to acknowledge the gift,
as if we were not in it or of it.

Take note of the proliferation of supermarkets and malls,
the altars of money.
They best describe the detour from grace.

Keep track of the errors of our forgetfulness; the fog
steals our children while we sleep.

Flowers of rage spring up in the depression.
Monsters are born there of nuclear anger.

Trees of ashes wave good-bye to good-bye and the map appears
    to disappear.

We no longer know the birds here,
how to speak to them by their personal names.

Once we knew everything in this lush promise.

What I am telling you is real and is printed in a warning
on the map. Our forgetfulness stalks us, walks the earth
behind us, leaving a trail of paper diapers,
needles and wasted blood.

An imperfect map will have to do, little one.

The place of entry is the sea of your mother's blood,
your father's small death
as he longs to know himself in another.

There is no exit.

The map can be interpreted through the wall of the intestine—
a spiral on the road of knowledge.

You will travel through the membrane of death, smell cooking
from the encampment where our relatives make a feast of
fresh deer meat and corn soup, in the Milky Way.

They have never left us; we abandoned them for science.

And when you take your next breath as we enter the fifth world
there will be no X, no guidebook with words you can carry.

Joy Harjo

You will have to navigate by your mother's voice,
renew the song she is singing.

Fresh courage glimmers from planets.

And lights the map printed with the blood of history, a map
you will have to know by your intention,
by the language of suns.

When you emerge note the tracks of the monster slayers
where they entered the cities of artificial light
and killed what was killing us.

You will see red cliffs. They are the heart, contain the ladder.

A white deer will come to greet you when the last human
climbs from the destruction.

We were never perfect.

Yet, the journey we make together is perfect on this earth
who was once a star
and made the same mistakes as humans.

We might make them again, she said.

Crucial to finding the way is this: there is no beginning or end.

You must make your own map.

◆　◆　◆　◆　◆

I WILL NOT NAME ALL the teachers. Some do not want to be named, and some remain nameless. Others would not call me a student because we were standing apart from each other, or we were friends, or both—yet, they taught me. Those stern and unforgiving teachers were the toughest and were the ones from whom I probably learned the most.

Some teachers are places, are oceans and mountains. Some are insects crawling the earth or flying. I am still learning. It is never ending, this inner search for knowledge.

◆　◆　◆　◆　◆

WHEN IT WAS TIME TO leave O'ahu, after nearly twelve years living on that island in the Pacific, my spirit approached to speak to me. I sensed what it was going to ask me. I knew I couldn't escape what was going to be asked as I lay down on the cool of the ohia wood floor of my office in that home in Alewa Heights, with my favorite plumeria trees outside in the sundown direction. I paged through my life on that island I loved so much: the canoe racing; my favorite day of coming upon a conference of more than fifty sea turtles out near the sandbar at Kaneohe Bay and how that day I surfed and surfed a perfect wave break in my one-man canoe; my *kumu*, or teacher, of *lomilomi*; the chanting and poetry of that island that had made circles of leis around my spirit. The house was quiet, with Hawaiian music playing low in the next room. Tradewinds were blowing through the open screened windows. The lights of Honolulu were stars on the ocean of night.

I told my spirit, "Please don't ask me to leave. I cannot let go of these waters, these lands, these people."

Joy Harjo

Me with my grandchildren Desiray and Tayo. Photo by Rainy
Dawn Ortiz.

You always have a choice, and when it is truly your guidance,
your spirit, there is no force. I was shown, like a quick sketch,
what would happen if I stayed. I saw a diminishment of my oppor-
tunities; I would wilt, like a plant without the proper nourishment. I would be unhappy with my choice. And if I returned to my
mainland home, I would be aligned with my path. I saw a bright-
ness, a happiness. I knew before I even saw the flickering shape of
possible outcomes what I had to do.

Just because you know what you are supposed to do and agree
to the path doesn't guarantee that it will be easy. Leaving that

island and those waters and my home there was one of the hardest things. But it was time. I missed my family in New Mexico, I missed those back-and-forth journeys to Oklahoma I have made ever since I first left for Indian school.

I had to go home.

♦ ♦ ♦ ♦ ♦

IT'S RAINING IN HONOLULU

There is a small mist at the brow of the mountain,
Each leaf of flower, of taro, tree, and bush shivers with ecstasy.
And the rain songs of all the flowering ones who have called for
    the rain
Can be found there, flourishing beneath the currents of singing.
Rain opens us, like flowers, or earth that has been thirsty for
    more than a season.
We stop all of our talking, quit thinking, to drink the mystery.
We listen to the breathing beneath our breathing.
We hear how the rain became rain, how we became human.
The wetness saturates and cleans everything, including the
    perpetrators
Of the second overthrow.
We will plant songs where there were curses.

♦ ♦ ♦ ♦ ♦

I HAD NEVER DREAMED OF pink dolphins, but a dream implanted itself in me when I was a child to go to the Amazon. I noticed it there in my spirit when I was about seven years old and

Joy Harjo

we had a school assignment to report on an animal. At that age I paid close attention to animals of the Amazon. For the assignment I chose anaconda. Even as I reported on and drew the huge snake, I could feel it moving through the water, and imagined how it must feel to be a snake that immense, even up to more than five hundred pounds. I felt how I preferred the water over land. Even now I can imagine how I imagined, the feel of the water current, and how the tremble of any walking mammal no matter how large or small stimulated my stomach muscles to find shelter or food. These anacondas are some of the largest snakes in the world. I knew one day I would get to that river. I didn't know how or when, but I could feel that river, and dreamed of the river animals.

A recurring dream through my forties and early fifties was this: I arrive at Iquitos, the Peruvian town that is the portal to the Amazon. I walk to a boat where I am greeted in Navajo. Navajo isn't the Native language. The indigenous people in the area speak Iquito, but this is a dream and there are all sorts of river, language, and image crossings in dreams. The same local Native man greets me every dream visit there.

Years later, my flight from Lima to Iquitos has mechanical problems and we make an emergency landing in Pucallpa. (A year or so later the same flight from Lima will crash in Pucallpa, killing several even as most passengers will survive and walk home into the jungle from the wreck.) Because I have missed the larger tour boat that routinely carries passengers to the camp, I am informed by the tourist agency I will be taken by a smaller conveyance. Bananas and mailbags are piled in the back. I am introduced to the man I am told will drive the boat there. I am disappointed that he is not the man I have seen in my dreams.

I am seated in the small boat, one passenger wide, and wait

for the loading to finish. Perched in the noisy jetty I can feel the waters of the Amazon surge and flow with the wake trails of water traffic. I smell gasoline and oil mixed with fish, earth, and water. I drip with humidity and the stress of travel. I muse on having stood in line at five that morning in the Lima airport, the man in line next to me with several boxes of roosters to ship. They crowed and crowed though there was no direct morning sun in the airport, as the man filled out paperwork.

Then the driver of the boat climbs in and turns to greet me. He is not the man I was just told will escort me, he is the same man I have met three times in my dreams, greeting me at the doorway to the Amazon.

As I reimagine that journey down the Amazon, I am emotional. I breathe deep to take in the feel of the water, the smell, the way the late afternoon sun cuts in and out of the windows in the boat to cross back and forth across my body, the feel of the river, the grandmother of all rivers of earth, like the largest snake, the anaconda, moving across the earth. I do not want to leave this feeling and I stay here for a while. I stop my word making. Here, the many-layered green, the waters so wide I cannot see across. I am a deep wave of water muscle, moving east always east to the mouth of the river, like the mouth of a large snake, swallowing and transforming all that enters into nourishment.

During that encampment we made many day and night trips. On one, as we traveled the big river, villagers stood and held an anaconda. It was seven to eight people long. We waved but did not stop. Maybe it was on this trip that we saw the pink dolphins. We stopped in the middle of the river and anchored at an island of plants and mudbanks. The driver stood up in the boat and called out for the dolphins in his language. I wondered what he told them, what he asked. Pink dolphins rose to the surface, they jumped and played around us, called out by the driver and the lure of fish snacks he carried.

To see the pink dolphins was like watching a herd of unicorns come over a hill toward us. They appeared as mythical creatures who were hidden far, far away where few people could find them, because for some humans, the greedy, to find them would be to destroy them.

I had not known there were pink dolphins in the world. In Oʻahu it was a special moment to paddle out and sight a school of dolphins. Joy, joy to watch the dolphin babies leaping and spinning with glee, their pink bellies sparking light.

As I write I wonder if this memory of river, snakes, dolphins, people, jungle will live only in my imagination, a beautiful, lush garden in the past to be wondered at by our grandchildren and great-grandchildren. It is the greedy who have been stealing land, burning it off with great fires that can be seen from satellites flying miles overhead. They are destroying these lungs of the earth for money. They destroy waters and lands as they suck up oil and other precious resources from the Amazon. They have even organized hunting expeditions to kill the indigenous peoples who live there and have been killing the leaders of those who take care of these lands. They are so empty and hungry from hate and greed they no longer remember they are the earth and will answer to earth. The pink dolphins are nearly extinct.

In 1990, more than ten years before that Amazonian journey, I attended a gathering of indigenous peoples. The western world was preparing to celebrate Columbus with Columbian Quincentenary events throughout the hemisphere in 1992. Native peoples wanted to make an assessment from those times forward to the times of seven generations beyond us. We gathered in a village not far outside Quito, Ecuador. We drove through clouds to get there. This was strictly a Native event. There were people from as far away as the Inupiaq in the Arctic, to tribal groups from Tierra del Fuego.

We were still reckoning with the violence and destruction set loose when Christopher Columbus sailed into our indigenous reality. He and his crew were welcomed by peoples in the West Indies who had never known weapons or violence. They sliced the tribal greeters with swords, enslaved the rest of the population, and took what they could from the lands rich in natural resources, including the young women for the sex trade.

One afternoon while taking a rest from meetings, as we gathered to sip coffee and soft drinks and to smoke, we watched with awe as a delegation of Amazonian tribal people walked up to the camp, barefoot, dressed in feathers and carrying spears. They had heard of the gathering, they told us through translators, and had come up to inform us of the destruction of their homes by the American oil companies. They reported how oil spills were killing their waters, their lands. They had never dealt with such forces and came to request assistance.

SILÊNCIO GUERREIRO

By Márcia Wayna Kambeba of the Kambeba people in Brazil

No território indígena
O silêncio é sabedoria milenar
Aprendemos com os mais velhos
A ouvir, mais que falar.

No silêncio da minha flecha
Resisti, não fui vencido
Fiz do silêncio a minha arma
Pra lutar contra o inimigo.

Silênciar é preciso,
Para ouvir com o coração,
A voz da Natureza
O choro do nosso chão.

O canto da mãe d'água
Que na dança com o vento
Pede que a respeite
Pois é fonte de sustento.

É preciso silenciar
Para pensar na solução
De frear o homem branco
E defender o nosso lar
Fonte de vida e beleza
Para nós, para a nação!

WARRIOR SILENCE

(Translation by Tiffany Higgins)

In Indigenous territory
Silence is ancient wisdom
We learn from the elders
To listen more than to speak

With my arrow's silence
I resisted, I wasn't conquered
From silence I formed my weapon
To battle the enemy.

You must grow quiet
To hear with the heart
The voice of Nature
The cry of our earth

The song of the Mother of the Water
Who in her dance with the wind
Asks we respect her
As the source of sustenance.

You must fall silent
To consider a solution
To halt the white man
And defend our dwelling
Source of life and beauty
For us, for the nation!

◆ ◆ ◆ ◆ ◆

WE WERE MORE THAN SIXTY poets on the stage of one of the world's largest poetry festivals, in Medellín, Colombia. We were asked to read one poem because there were so many poets. The amphitheater was packed with residents of the city—in that country poetry has a place in everyday living. Poems are recited there the same as popular songs are known and listened to here in this country. For a poet to be in a place where poetry is revered is a reverse reality, a little difficult to take in at first.

As each poet read, the audience drank in each word and phrase. Everyone moved in synch, poets and audience, taking in poetry and letting out appreciation in shouts and claps.

All the poets were seated on the stage together, which meant we were always in view of the audience. I was seated in the row of indigenous poets, and as usual, we sat close to the back. The performance was growing longer and longer because poets began adding more and more poems to their performances. After two hours we were getting tired and hungry as we waited to go on. No one had thought to bring snacks or water.

An indigenous poet from Colombia sat to my left. Sherwin Bitsui, a Navajo poet, was on my right. The poet from Colombia reached into his woven shoulder bag, pulled out his small stash of coca leaves, and offered us some, to help with the fatigue, the hunger. Sherwin and I were cautious in accepting. In our country the coca leaves had been colonized and force-mixed with ingredients to make a fine white powder that changed the character of the plant. In that processed form it harmed and was illegal. I had never seen natural coca leaves.

We opened our hands to graciously accept this gift. The poet gave each of us a palm of leaves. He instructed us to chew them. After we chewed them, we were no longer hungry. We moved through the rest of the reading without weariness.

When I held the leaves, I felt the presence of the plant, and saw how the indigenous people there had a relationship, an agreement with the plant. There was humbleness and respectfulness in the interaction, from the way the poet asked us, then gathered the leaves and placed them in our hands. And yet the plant had become an outlaw in our lands. The same happened with tobacco and corn. They were sent to help us, then abused with other ingredients and poisons, put into slavery to make money and feed addictions that kill.

I can still feel those leaves in my hand. They knew they were sacred; they were loved.

◆ ◆ ◆ ◆ ◆

MY FAVORITE ROOM EXISTS NOW only in the imagination. That's how I visit it these days. I turn left into the yard of the small adobe house and park near the corn patch, which is by the clothesline.

I look to see if the swallow's nest is still on the porch. Then I check to see if beaks are bobbing out of the nest, as the babies look to see if someone is coming to feed them.

I knock on the kitchen door and she lets me in, as she has done more times than I know, in many seasons of weather. It is always warm with sunlight. Dishes are drying on the side of the sink. Either she, her sister, or a niece gets me coffee. In later years she had a cane. We'd talk family, village, and Native community gossip. Sometimes we'd put on music and everyone danced. She distrusted computers. Said they stole people. Kept their attention from what mattered. We'd walk back through the small hallway, the neat living room decorated with Pendleton blankets and Indian rugs. There were baskets, potteries, and family pictures.

I remember visiting when her mother lived there. And during feast days when the house filled with tables of food and the commotion of serving, talking, and laughter.

We'd go to her special room, the place where the medicine box

Joy Harjo

lived, her herbs, the various items given to her by those she helped, and her altar.

She had a small shop in town where she worked. The numbers of street people, who were predominately Native, grew each year. She would feed them, find them clothes, and otherwise help any way that she could. She never turned anyone down who asked for help.

She always gave my children words and assistance in whatever they were studying or doing. My daughter stayed with her on weekends from Indian school when I lived out of town. Through the years they loved to visit her.

Many came to her from all over the world for her teachings that were rooted in her spiritual knowledge. She had many invitations to travel and teach, but she did not want to put herself out that way. Her spiritual energy was a healing light and people were drawn to it, to her stories. Her pueblo roots were powerful anchors to the land.

Her house was thick with song resonance. Through her eyes I came to see that all is spiritual and either we move about respectfully within it, or we are lost.

One day we went back to her room and she pulled out her drum. We sang the song she had been given when we had gone to the Sandia Mountains for cedar. Her hands were the color of the drum. They appeared to be made out of the same earth. She later gave me that drum. When I sing that song for the cedar and what it brings, it reminds me of the spiritual path that sometimes appears dim in the smoke of historical deception.

One of my favorite memories in this life will be sitting outside near the corn patch on a bench, with my daughter and her little boys, my grandsons, waiting for her to drive up. The boys squat in the sandy dirt, running it through their hands. Our love for them plays about their shoulders. It catches the light of the love with which the corn was planted, with which the yard and house were tended, with which her life was lived.

Mvto, Batheu. Herkem.

✦ ✦ ✦ ✦ ✦

AND THEN POET WARRIOR BECAME a teacher.

Part Six

SUNSET

FROG IN A DRY RIVER

When you talk with the dead
You can only go as far as the edge of the bank.

I heard more than one frog singing.

She came to me more than once in dead
Sleep. We used to drink, and she doesn't want anyone to tell.

I met the king of the frogs once perched on the lip of the ditch.

The water had been let down for the summer for the crops
And we camped out nearby, with singers, the ones who knew
The oldest songs.

Said the frog as he pitched his favorite pillow behind his
Aching back

It's hard getting old, and soon we will all be dead.
He sang as we sat together and watched
The human traffic hiking by.

The jealousy beast lives too among us frogs, he mused.

I watched it going across in a yellow boat, toward the
Land of the dead. It had six rowers to haul the sharp-tongued.

We are never free of ourselves, not here or in froggy heaven.

Then the river spoke up. She'd had enough of the disregard,
The theft. *I'm not dead*, she said.

I wanted to learn a song from the frog. The frog leaped in, and
My mind followed. I started this poem.

To argue with the living is hard enough, forget the dead.
I will end here, instead.

✦　✦　✦　✦　✦

I HAD MOVED INTO MY mother's sewing room at the end of
the summer, to assist her as she completed lung cancer treatments.
She was vigorous, talkative, always moving, and continued to eat
whatever she wanted. She still used a walker for getting around,
though she'd stubbornly ditch it, then have to return to it within a
few minutes. She didn't like anyone else in her home looking out
for her, yet she needed someone there. She was independent, ter-
ritorial, and bossy.

The first time I drove her to a cancer treatment she looked over
at me, as I maneuvered through a busy intersection, and noted that
it had been a long time since we had had any sort of time together.
We were going to get to know each other in a way we hadn't since I
fled from home as a teenager to Indian school. Her words acknowl-
edged the deep-water of the unspoken, stuck between us.

I say "fled," though she and my stepfather drove me to New
Mexico. With each mile I felt freer and freer, and after my mother
checked me in to Indian school and they left me and my footlocker
of belongings at the dorm, I never looked back. My mother and I
wrote letters. There were phone calls, and my usual summer vis-
its for stomp dance season. I did not always understand her, but I
respected and loved her.

For most of those years I was not allowed home to see her. I
was banished by my stepfather because I had told the truth about

how his behavior had hurt all of us in a letter to her that he illegally opened. He opened all of her mail. He monitored all of her calls, any trips outside the house. He banished me, and she went along with it. I would have to find her at work to see her, and we'd visit in the backrooms of kitchens.

After he died, several years later, I was once again welcome in her home, but her compulsive smoking made it difficult to stay there. She had been smoking since she was around ten years old. She quit smoking ten years before her lung cancer diagnosis. The ritual of smoking had been her closest companion all those years.

Tobacco is one of our sacred plants. It has powers, ways to help humans. When it is colonized, grown and then processed with additives, it loses the strength of its healing properties and gains the power to addict. I was taught to use tobacco as a way to open the door to the spiritual path, to signal to those in the spiritual realm that I am here and listening, thinking of them too. It is a way to begin a conversation, a connection, to open the door to prayer. Smokers usually circle together innately. There's visiting, a kind of communion as smoke winds through the winds, between and around them.

After my mother's cancer treatments, she always wanted to go eat at a restaurant somewhere. Her appetite never waned, and she would often order two desserts. Or we would go shopping for groceries. Every supermarket now has a plant section. One afternoon she pointed out a large pot of bright flowers she wanted. I carried them out and loaded them into the car, then carried the flowers to her porch and set them down where she instructed. It was then I heard the other plants nearby making a ruckus. I couldn't believe I was actually hearing them. They didn't speak English, yet I knew exactly what they were saying.

"We don't want that plant over here!!"

"Well then," I said, in the part of my mind in which the flowers were speaking to me, "you're being rude. And this plant doesn't need to be next to you."

I moved the plant elsewhere on her porch to a place where they welcomed and greeted the new family member.

Since then, I am more sensitive to plant politics, and to their individual differences within species. Each has a kind of personality, an individual presence.

Our physical living is held together by plant sacrifice. We eat, wear, and are sheltered by plants and plant material. Nearly all of our medicines are plant-derived. We need to take time with them, get to know them. It's as one of the elders from a nearby pueblo told me once when she came to visit. She admired the two aloe vera plants who took up a large part of the living room, as they basked in the sunlight filtered through the skylight. They loved her attention. "These are the knowledge bearers. They are the ones we need to be listening to, not your computer, your internet that is pulling you into a world that will never feed you, only make you hungrier," she told me.

So now, because of her words, my mother, and my relationship with my plants, I listen more closely.

◆   ◆   ◆   ◆   ◆

I HAD GOTTEN TO BED fairly late. I was in the final edits of my first memoir, *Crazy Brave,* and stayed up working. My mother would always wake me up near five A.M., as she often did when I was a child, to keep her company. It was the same now, years later, as I stayed with her while she battled cancer. The next morning, I startled awake about four A.M. and quietly walked across the living room to her bedroom to check on her breathing. She was breathing shallowly, and asleep. I crawled back into my pallet and dreamed. In the dream my mother was dying. I saw her spirit lifting away and reached for her. I awoke in alarm to bright sunlight. I had overslept. My mother usually woke me by now. I found her in the hallway with her walker. She was crying out with what little breath she had,

"I can't breathe, I can't breathe."

Such a cry from your life giver is primal terror territory. I panicked, yet found tremendous control somewhere within and thought to give my mother her inhaler. Then I calmly told her that I would call her hospice worker.

Her hospice worker told me to take a deep breath, then walked me with her voice over to my mother's medications.

"Give her the pill for anxiety," she told me, "and one of the morphine. I will be there as soon as I can."

I found the pills and gave them to my mother with water, followed with a bite of banana to soothe her stomach from them. I very, very carefully walked her to her bed, arranged her, spread the covers carefully over her shoulders as the pills took hold. Then I quickly called my sister, told her to come over as soon as possible. In retrospect, I didn't know why I urgently felt the need to call my sister and get her over there; something in me knew she needed to be there. The hospice worker was on her way.

I went back in to check on my mother and placed one hand on her shoulder and the other on her hip as she lay on her side in the bed, the same side I always start out sleeping on. I took a deep breath in, pulling in love and assistance, and allowed that love to move through me, to her. I prayed for her. I told my mother that my sister was on the way. Her body responded with happiness. I told my mother in rhythm:

Breathe in, breathe out. Breathe in, breathe out.
Let it go, let it go.

I breathed with her. I felt her heart in a kind of a leap, not like a run, but a gentle movement up, then down and under. I realized later I had felt that same motion only once before in someone I was helping who was dying in the veterans' hospital in O'ahu, a Mvskoke tribal member named Bill Tiger from Broken Arrow.

I told my mother I loved her. Her last words would be, "I love you too."

Breathe in. Breathe out.

I lifted my hands to allow the light through me to her.

Later I would realize I was midwifing my mother through to her next life.

Let it go, let it go.

The hospice worker rang the doorbell and asked if she should call an ambulance. Though she knew the answer, she was required by law to ask.

"No," I told her. My mother had made it clear what she wanted.

She came in, took one look at my mother—who did not look like a typical dying-of-cancer patient—and remarked that my mother most likely had caught something on one of her trips out of the house. My sister had taken her to the state fair, where she'd been able to have one of her favorite Indian tacos. Our mother would not stay home as the hospice team wanted.

I counted heartbeats while the hospice worker checked her other vitals. We straightened my mother on the bed. My mother kept sleeping.

My sister came in with my niece. The three of us surrounded her on the bed when the hospice worked called out in surprise, "She's going!"

We watched our mother take her last breath. Then she was gone from us.

❖ ❖ ❖ ❖ ❖

WASHING MY MOTHER'S BODY

I never got to wash my mother's body when she died.
I return to take care of her in memory.
That's how I make peace when things are left undone.
I go back and open the door.
I step in to make my ritual. To do what should have been done,
what needs to be fixed so that my spirit can move on,
So that the children and grandchildren are not caught in a knot
Of regret they do not understand.

I find the white enamel pan she used to bathe us
when we were babies.
I turn the faucet on and hold my hand under the water
until it is warm, the temperature one uses to wash an infant.
I find a clean washcloth in a stack of washcloths.
She had nothing in her childhood.
She made sure she had plenty of everything
when she grew up and made her own life.
Her closets were full of pretty dresses,

so many she had not time to wear them all.
They were bought by the young girl who wore the same flour
     sack dress
to school every day, the one she had to wash out every night,
and hang up to dry near the wood stove.

I pick up the bar of soap from her sink,
the same soap she used yesterday morning to wash her face.
When she looked in the mirror, did she know it would be her last
     sunrise?
I move over pill bottles, a clock radio on the table by the bed,
a pen and set down the pan. I straighten the blankets over her,
to keep her warm, for dignity.
I start with her face. Her face is unlined even two months before
her eightieth birthday. She was known for her beauty,
and when younger passed for the Cherokee
that she was through her mother and her mother's mother
all the way back to time's beginning.
My mother had the iron pot given to her by her Cherokee mother,
whose mother gave it to her, given to her by the U.S. government
on the Trail of Tears.

She grew flowers in it.

As I wash my mother's face, I tell her
how beautiful she is, how brave, how her beauty and bravery
live on in her grandchildren. Her face is relaxed, peaceful.
Her earth memory body has not left yet,
but when I see her the next day, embalmed and in the casket
in the funeral home, it will be gone.
Where does it go?

Joy Harjo

It is heavier than the spirit who lifted up and flew.
I think of it making the rounds to every place it has loved to say
    good-bye.
Good-bye to the house where I brought my babies home, she sings.
Good-bye to June's Bar where I was the shuffleboard queen.

I cannot say good-bye yet.
I will never say good-bye.

I lift up each arm to wash. Her hands still wear her favorite rings.
She loved her body and decorated it with shiny jewelry,
with creams and makeup.
I am tender over that burn scar on her arm,
From when she cooked at the place with the cruel boss
who insisted she reach her hand into the Fryolator to clean it.
She had protested it was still hot and suffered a deep burn.
That scar always reminded me of her coming in
from working long hours in restaurants,
her uniform drenched with sweat, determination, and exhaustion.
Once she came home and I was burning up with a fever.
She pulled out the same pan I am dipping the washcloth in now,
only she's added rubbing alcohol, to bring the fever down.
She washes tenderly, tells me about how her friend Chunkie
left her husband again, how she knows her old boss,
a Jewish woman who treated her kindly,
has cancer. She doesn't know how she knows;
she just knows.
She doesn't tell me that—
I find it in a journal she has left me,
a daybook in which she has written notes
for me to find when she is gone.

I wash her neck and lift the blankets to move down to her heart.
I thank her body for carrying us through the tough story,
through the violence of my father, and her second husband.

The story is all there, in her body, as I wash her to prepare her
to be let down into earth and return all stories to the earth.
My body memories rise up as I wash.
I recall carrying my two children, rocking them,
and feeding them from my body.
How I knew myself as beloved Earth, in that body.

I uncover my mother's legs.
I remember the varicose veins that swelled like rivers
when my mother would get off a long shift of standing and
    cooking.
They carried more than a woman should carry.
A woman should be honored like a queen,
traditionally we treated our women with that kind of respect,
my Creek husband tells me.
Ha, I laugh and ask him, "then why aren't you cooking my dinner?"
I wash her feet, caress them.
You will have some rest now, I tell my mother,
even as I know my mother was never one for resting.
I cover her.

I make the final wring of the washcloth and drape it over the pan.
I brush my mother's hair and kiss her forehead.
I ask the keepers of the journey to make sure her travel is safe and
    sure.
I ask the angels, whom she loved and with whom she spoke
    frequently,

to take her home, but wait, not before I find her favorite perfume.
Then I sing her favorite song, softly.
I don't know the name of the song, just a few phrases,
one of those old homemade heartbreak songs
where there's a moment of happiness
wound through—

and then I let her go.

❖　❖　❖　❖　❖

THAT FIRST BIRTHDAY AFTER MY mother's death I was heading to the airport. As I drove in the early morning dark to catch my flight the van suddenly filled up with the smell of pancakes my mother used to make, then I heard her singing me "Happy Birthday," in her distinctive and funny way of singing it. That's how I knew it was her.

That's how I was being taught, there is no time, there is no space.

❖　❖　❖　❖　❖

I MOVED BACK TO OKLAHOMA after my mother passed from this earth. I returned to my family here, to my Muscogee Creek people where I belonged, just as my spirit told me I would years ago. I married Owen Sapulpa, a Muscogee Creek citizen whom I had met years ago when we were young Native activists working for justice in New Mexico at the National Indian Youth Council. I returned with him to *Oce Vpofv* ceremonial grounds, my family's home grounds, though I had long been made welcome at *Tvlahasse Wvkokaye* ceremonial grounds. I finally made it home.

My husband, Owen, and I, watching my niece's lacrosse game. Tulsa, 2019. Photo by Margaret Barrows.

And then there we were, just like the Old Ones, my cousin George Coser Jr. and me, in the same manner my aunt Lois used to visit with her cousin George Sr. all those years ago. For years, my cousin and I visited mostly on the phone. And now because I'm home we visit in person. Before the diabetes got so bad, he'd drive over and I'd cook for him while he told me stories. He likes my biscuits. I now visit him at his place in Mounds. We talk about everything from tribal and national politics, to family stories. I tell

Me and my cousin George at the opening of the National Museum of the American Indian, 2004, Washington, D.C. Photo by Lurline Wailana McGregor.

him about my former band member who, when he was a judge at a neighbor Pueblo community, demanded the whole tribe come in for counseling. We speak of the philosophical precepts of our people, our genealogy, the meanings of songs and words in our language. There are so many stories, like how his friend invited him to lunch then took him to a shelter where they were feeding free meals to the homeless, or that time we stomp danced the whole route for the opening of the National Museum of the American Indian in Washington, D.C., and so it goes and will continue as long as there is memory.

Every day at this sunset place in my life, I grow more and more excited at the thought of seeing my relatives, my teachers once again. I hear them in these words. They tell me that they never left.

◆　◆　◆　◆　◆

Poet Warrior stood at the doorway of time.
She held the child of the seventh generation in her arms
Adjusted the soft blanket to see her face
To glimpse what this one was bringing with her to share,
In the way she took every child, grandchild, and great-grandchild
Into her arms to welcome them, to bless them
During her time walking on the earth.
Poet Warrior smiled as she thought: she looks Japanese.
She resembled her daughter Rainy.
Poet Warrior sang into the baby a song that would give her
      strength,
And sustenance, would always call her ancestors to stand behind
      her
No matter the trials, no matter history and heartbreak—
Then she walked with her into time
To deliver the baby to the earth story that needed her.

Notes

MY TRIBAL NATION IS OFFICIALLY called the Muscogee (Creek) Nation. The landmark Supreme Court decision in the case of *McGirt v. Oklahoma* on July 9, 2020, confirmed that we are the Muscogee (Creek) Nation Reservation. We are also known as *Mvskoke* people, or the *Mvskokvlke.*

I reluctantly am going along with italicizing non-English words. Our indigenous language preceded English. I considered rendering the English in italics and the *Mvskoke* words in plain, regular type style (which is known as Roman).

Indigenous peoples within the boundaries of the United States use many terms for ourselves depending on generation, education, and geographical place. Generally, we use our tribal nations as identification. And as members within our nations we identify by clan systems, tribal towns, moieties, and/or bands. The collective term for indigenous nations was, and still is for some of us, "Indian," "American Indian," and colloquially sometimes "skins." The term "Native American" came into prominence out of the academic realm in the late eighties. I've resisted it and prefer the term "Native Nations" or "Indigenous" or even just "Native."

Acknowledgments

THERE ARE MANY TO ACKNOWLEDGE in the making of this memoir. I will start with the Tulsa Artist Fellowship, which gave me a place to live, a studio, time, and a community within which to work, right next to the Oklahoma Jazz Hall of Fame. The Jazz Hall is always supportive. They have given me space and support to perform and rehearse many of the poems/songs within this memoir. I thank the Atlantic Center for the Arts in New Smyrna Beach, Florida, for their generosity of a cottage and time during the most potent moment of the creation of this memoir. The Guggenheim Foundation supported the writing of this memoir with a fellowship. Their support and acknowledgment came in perfect timing.

I appreciate those who helped with this manuscript, from the first raw version to the most recent revisions. They include LeAnne Howe, Laura Coltelli, Sharon Oard Warner, Melissa Pritchard-Schley, Loren Khan, Dunya Mikhail, Barrett Martin and Lisette Garcia, and Haleigh Bush. And especially Jennifer Elise Foerster, who listened as I read the manuscript aloud and provided insight and assistance through the whole of the writing. For Elise Paschen, whose mother, much like mine in presence and urgency, tried to take over her poetry sequence. Mvto, Esperanza Spaulding, who took these pages to heart and sang her responses. And gratitude to Sven Haakanson for his detailed help in one of my favorite stories in the story field involving the will of culture to live. Mvto to Rosemary McCombs Maxey for the Mvskoke language translations, the willingness to share and teach our language. And to my cousin George Coser Jr., who also shares generously with anyone who wants to know our culture.

I remain especially grateful to the poet, writer, and my editor at Norton, Jill Bialosky, who has been here with me nearly the whole of my publishing journey, all the way from *The Woman Who Fell from the Sky*. And deep gratitude for Kathy Anderson, who fiercely guards the stories, the poems; and for Anya Backlund, my booking agent, who is my rudder as I travel about in real or virtual time. And there you are Rob Casper, my dancing partner, the keeper of poets, thank you for your belief in poetry, in all the poets.

Mvto, mvto, mvto, mvto to my familial, poetry, music, and teacher ancestors. They are many. Only a few are named specifically in this memoir. They helped shaped my story, and the way that it appears in the woven narrative of this book. And my family that ranges far and wide from here in Tulsa, Oklahoma, to all over the world. I want to remember my stepsister/second mother, Sandy Aston, whose story in my life is absent in these pages, but who saved me often in my growing-up years. She still walks alongside me, though she left this earth a few years before. Without her I would not be here. Mvto for the stories, the songs, and how we keep going no matter the challenges.

Finally, a special acknowledgment of my best friend, partner, husband, children-picker-upper, animal whisperer, stomp dancer Owen Chopoksa Sapulpa. You inspire me all days.

Credits

57 "The Lord Is My Shepherd," Psalm 23, King James Version of the Bible.

66 Harjo, Joy. "The Life of Beauty." *New York Times*, December 7, 2019.

87 Harjo, Joy. "How to Write a Poem in a Time of War" from *An American Sunrise: Poems* by Joy Harjo. Copyright © 2019 by Joy Harjo. Used by permission of W. W. Norton &Company, Inc.

93 Harjo, Joy. "For Calling the Spirit Back from Wandering the Earth in Its Human Feet" from *Conflict Resolution for Holy Beings: Poems* by Joy Harjo. Copyright © 2015 by Joy Harjo. Used by permission of W. W. Norton & Company, Inc.

99 Harjo, Joy. "Sunrise" from *Conflict Resolution for Holy Beings: Poems* by Joy Harjo. Copyright © 2015 by Joy Harjo. Used by permission of W. W. Norton & Company, Inc.

110 Harjo, Joy. "For Alva Benson, and For Those Who Have Learned to Speak" from *She Had Some Horses* by Joy Harjo. Copyright © 2008, 1983 by Joy Harjo. Used by permission of W. W. Norton & Company, Inc.

113 p'Bitek, Okot. *Song of Lawino, Song of Ocol*. Heineman Educational Publishers, African Writers Series, 1984. Reprinted by permission of Waveland Press, Inc. from p'Bitek: *Song of Lawino and Song of Ocol*. Long Grove, IL: Waveland Press, Inc., © 1967; reissued 2013. All rights reserved.

128 Harjo, Joy. "A Postcolonial Tale" from *The Woman Who Fell from the Sky* by Joy Harjo. Copyright © 1994 by Joy Harjo. Used by permission of W. W. Norton & Company, Inc.

139 Pepper, Jim. "Witchi Tai To." Jim Pepper, "Water spirit . . . ," reprinted with the permission of James Pepper Henry.

139 Harjo, Joy. "Stomp All Night." *I Pray for My Enemies* (Mekko Productions, Inc.). 2021

143 Lorca, Federico García. "Of the Dark Doves" from *Poet in Spain* by Federico García Lorca—New Translations by Sarah Arvio, copyright © 2017 by Sarah Arvio (translation, selection, intro-

PHOTOGRAPHS

12 Lois Harjo, Artist in Residence, Southern Methodist University 1935
30 My father, Allen W. Foster, Jr., as a boy